f

First published in Great Britain in 1999 by Fusion
Press a division of Satin Publications Limited.

Fusion Press,
a division of
Satin Publications Limited
20 Queen Anne Street
London W1M 0AY
Email: sheenadewan@compuserve.com

Cover Image: Nikolai Globe
Layout: Justine Hounam
Printed and bound by The Bath Press Ltd.

©1999 John Carson
ISBN: 1-901250-36-9

Beer and Bagels for Breakfast

John Carson

About the Author

John Carson was born in Edmonton, London, in 1969 and was destined to be a traveller after his first unsupervised trip along a Cornish beach at the age of two. He left school at 16 with six 'O' Levels and started work at a stockbroking firm as a messenger and coffee machine cleaner. After attending night school, he qualified as a share dealer during the trade boom of the late 1980's when he blew his wages on a backpacking trip around Australia, Bangkok and Singapore. Money well spent.

Further hedonistic trips have ensued around Europe, Canada, Israel and Egypt interspersed with mundane jobs in telesales, taxi driving and a famous pharmaceutical company to raise funds for travelling.

At the age of 24 he realised that time was getting on if he wanted to be a writer, and so went back to college for two years where he gained 3 'A' Levels, training in journalism and a crap beard that was shaved off almost immediately.

John started his journalism career on a business magazine at the age of 26, and currently works as an Editor on an international security magazine where he totally abuses his professional position to enjoy all expenses paid business trips abroad. He married his Canadian wife, Rebecca, in May 1999 and has two goldfish and a spider that lives in the car.

Dedication

This book is dedicated to Mum & Dave, Dad, Jayne, Rebecca, Jennifer, all my friends and family including Jim and family including Jim & Fabienne, Jonathan, John(Slap), Lucky, Smokey and Bunny.

A special mention for Phil & Anat, Gerald and Assat(DJ) who lived these experiences with me.

Acknowledgements

Many thanks to Paul & Mark Sheehan for their advice over a curry on 'when to chop and when to stop'.

Author's Note

The majority of names (people and places) have been changed to protect the drunks.

x

Contents

MAY

Sunday 3 May

12.30pm: I swear even my dog Smokey had a tear in her eye as I turned and bid farewell to my family. I had checked my rucksack and hand luggage at least fifty times, and they both seemed to weigh a tonne. One final look to see if I had remembered all the essential items – passport, traveller's cheques, plane tickets, radio cassette player, condoms...

5pm: Sitting on the plane waiting for take-off. Great – there's a security alert, and all the baggage had to be taken off the plane and counted. I sneaked a look at the man's passport sitting next to me, and things suddenly took a worrying turn – he's from Iran. Shit.

6.30pm: Eventually we took off, and I peered out of the window as Old Blighty slipped away, as we headed for the Holy Land.

Time for a can of in-flight lager. Or six.

Monday 4 May

I arrived at Ben-Gurion Airport, Tel Aviv at one in the morning (Israel is two hours ahead of England). When I stepped off the plane, the first thing that hit me was the oppressive heat. My head throbbed and my throat was as dry as a hedgehog's arse – but that's what you get from drinking cheap airline beer I suppose. I queued for 30 minutes to obtain my tourist visa that would last me three months before having to renew it. I couldn't help but notice how many airport security staff there were, checking litter bins for bombs and looking out for any trouble. I also noticed how beautiful the Israeli girls were. The adrenaline from the long journey had worn off slightly, and I was beginning to feel weary – it was time to find a place to stay for the night. Luckily, regular buses run between the airport and the city.

I checked my street plan of Tel Aviv and got off at Ha'arkon Street, right by the beach. It's a fairly seedy area and I noticed a few prostitutes hanging around. I was far too tired to hunt and haggle for a cheap hostel, so I checked into a dingy hotel, which cost me sixty sheckels, or about L8 for a single room. I had roughly L1200 to see me through the year, but I didn't mind splashing out for my first night.

Grabbing my cassette player and a couple of beers from reception, I headed down to the beach for a fantastic first night – lazing in a deck chair, watching the ocean, drinking cold beer and listening to 'Still Got The Blues' by Gary Moore. Hanging out in the Holy Land.

10am: I slept like a log last night – it must be the sea air. The temptation to laze around on the beach all day was strong, but I had a mission; I had to attend to the very reason why I came here in the first place – I needed to find a kibbutz to stay on.

The kibbutz volunteer main office in Tel Aviv is situated in Ha'arkon Street, so I didn't have far to walk. It took me a while to find, though, as the office wasn't very well sign posted.

Upstairs, there were seven young travellers in the waiting room: two blonde girls from Denmark
(please God, let us be on the same kibbutz), three loud blokes from the US and a German couple – every one of us 'kibbutz virgins'.

We started chatting about what we expected from Israel. The Danish girls wanted to 'pick oranges and learn the language...'; the German couple wanted to 'experience the interesting culture of another nation...'; the Yanks wanted to 'lay as much pussy as possible, man.'

Eventually my turn came. The woman who spoke to me was very efficient and a bit abrupt when she asked for a fee of one hundred shekels. I thought this was a bit much, considering I had already paid a fee in London. I showed her my papers from the kibbutz office in Golders Green, and I signed a form consenting to have an AIDS test once on the kibbutz.

I had some choice as to which area of Israel I could go to, because I wasn't part of an organised group. My motto has always been, 'the hotter the better', so I opted for the south of the country.

The woman told me that my destination would be Kibbutz Naloz. This, she told me, was situated about two miles from the Gaza Strip.

Hang on a minute, isn't that the very same place that I watch on the news where they throw large, deadly, hurtful rocks and shoot each other? Oh well – in for a shekel, in for a pound.

Spent the rest of the day on the beach turning lobster red. A Canadian tourist was killed on this stretch of beach a few years back, when an Arab bomb exploded in a bin, but I tried not to think too much about that.

May

Tuesday 5 May

I set off at ten o'clock, sweat already rising. Shorts, shades and rucksack on, I made my way to the Central Bus Station. Whoever invented the word 'chaos' must have drawn his inspiration from this place; male and female soldiers were everywhere, going to their various bases and postings, most of them carrying a weapon. Locals hurried in every direction, dodging the buses crammed in the station, whilst dodgy pop music blared out from market stalls and small shops. Mouth-watering smells wafted in the air: fresh bread, kebabs, bagels, cakes and hot coffee.

I eventually found my number 363 bus down a side street. The driver told me the journey to Kibbutz Naloz would take about two hours, so it was a great relief to find the buses (more like comfortable coaches) are air-conditioned in Israel. Sitting at the back of a bus driven by an Israeli, is like being on a roller coaster. Looking down the aisle of the bus and through the windscreen while the bus swung around tight corners left me feeling distinctly nervous; it was the first time I'd been on a bus that overtook vehicles on a blind bend! I was hoping that I hadn't travelled all this way just to end up in a road crash. I had already managed that in England in my gold two-litre Ford Capri, during my boy-racer phase.

Eventually I reached the junction where I had to get off. The driver shouted back to me in Hebrew and indicated with his thumb that this was my stop. Gathering my belongings, I staggered off the bus, looked around and quickly realised that I was in a desert. A sign told me in both Hebrew and English that the Kibbutz Naloz was three miles down a sun-baked road. There were fields all around me, and a tractor worked away in the distance. That tractor, and the odd lizard, were the only signs of life. 'Well you wanted the heat,' I murmured to myself and started to walk through the shimmering haze towards the kibbutz.

Fifteen minutes passed by – but not one car. My mouth was as dry as sandpaper and I was kicking myself for not buying water before leaving Tel Aviv.

Just then, the sweet sound of a car engine reached my ears. I quickly stuck out my forefinger to thumb a lift. I remembered reading in a guide that using a thumb translates as 'fuck you' – which is not a reliable way of persuading people to stop for a stranger. Hitching is a very normal thing in Israel. If an army vehicle drives

past a hitchhiking soldier and ignores them, they are normally repri-
manded.

The car stopped and I glanced at the colour of the number plate.
Yellow plates mean that the vehicle is Israeli registered, and blue
ones are Arab-registered, which could be a bit risky for thumbing a
lift.

There was one civilian driver and two soldiers in the car. They
offered to drop me at the kibbutz, which was music to my ears. By
that point, my trainers felt like they were melting onto my feet.

A few minutes later I was at journey's end – the front gates of
Kibbutz Naloz lay before me.

My first thought was that it looked like a big park, with grass,
trees, water sprinklers and a perimeter road. There were also rows
of cream bungalows with red roofs. Outside one of these houses, I
spotted some people sitting around a table, so I walked over and
introduced myself as a new volunteer.

Without further question, they took me inside their house and
gave me some coke and cake. Their hospitality was heartening after
my long journey, making me feel very welcome even though I was a
complete stranger.

They telephoned the volunteers' accommodation block and
Anne, an English volunteer, came over to greet me and get me
settled in. She was from Manchester and had been living on the
kibbutz for about three months.

She took me to where the volunteers stayed. There were two
accommodation blocks, one in front of the other, with a lawn in
between. I was then introduced to six other tanned volunteers:
Jenny (Manchester), Linda (Liverpool), Ben and Peter (South
Africa), Mette and Dorte (Sweden).

Like me, they were all in their early 20s except for the two
Swedish girls who were both eighteen.

We chatted for a few minutes before I went into my room for the
first time. This was the moment when I thought I had made a big
mistake in coming to Israel.

I stared at four blank walls – well, not exactly blank as they were
smothered in graffiti. There was one bed (at least I was lucky to
have a room to myself) and a wardrobe. I half expected a jailer to
walk past and tell me to slop out my cell. The communal shower
and toilet was outside, at the end of the corridor.

It struck me that the only way to achieve any luxury would be to grab other volunteers' furniture when they left. I sensed that being a volunteer was going to involve basic laws of the jungle.

7pm: Official kibbutz dinner time. I walked into the dining room and people stared at me as if I was a rasher of bacon. Talk about a way of sizing up strangers! I had missed the main meal of the day, which is held at noon. On offer now was soup, toast, tea, coffee and evidently more salad than in a rabbit's wet dream.

I met the volunteer leader, an Israeli girl/woman/cow (please delete) called Beatrice. It was obvious that she didn't take any shit, and liked to remind the volunteers that she was the big cheese – numero uno – as far as we were concerned. I got the distinct feeling that it was best to stay in her good books or risk losing my bagels. She brought me some work clothes and told me that I had the following day off as I was a new arrival.

Beatrice briefed me about the kibbutz. There were roughly four hundred members living together on a big commune. Everybody shared the work equally and had their food and housing provided free. It was the same deal for volunteers.

There were a variety of jobs available to volunteers, including working on the dishwasher (which would be my first job), looking after cows and chickens, farming, factory work and fruit picking. Israel has a six day working week, lasting from Sunday to Friday, and we had to work six to eight hours depending on the job we were assigned, although we were given two extra days off a month which we could accumulate and save for trips if we wished. There was a free volunteer trip organised by the kibbutz every three months to a specific destination, such as Jerusalem. Volunteers earned 'pocket money' of one hundred shekels a month, and free aerogrammes. Added extras included the Kibbutz Naloz swimming pool, which opens in June, and a pub/disco open on Friday nights for members only, and Saturday nights for the paying public as well.

11pm: One way ticket to sleep city...

Wednesday 6 May

I explored the kibbutz grounds and tried to get my bearings. I wasn't sure that I would ever be able to find my way around the place. There were paths leading off in all directions, tree-lined alleys and various short cuts. A wire fence surrounded the perimeter road, and gazing across the fields, I could see the outskirts of Gaza City two miles away. I don't know if I expected to hear the sounds of gunfire and explosions, but it was deadly quiet – only the sounds of crickets and flies for company.

The swimming pool was locked so I climbed over the gate. It was empty and full of tree branches and deck chairs. It would certainly have to be cleaned – and filled – before it could be opened.

Continuing my walk took me on to the cowsheds. I chatted to one of the members working there who told me that the dairy contained three hundred and fifty cows, and they all had to be milked three times a day. These guys started work at 4am but used a shift system. Next, the chicken sheds. They smelt absolutely disgusting, but I ventured inside, nevertheless. The sheds were about the length of a football pitch and half as wide. The sound of thousands of tiny yellow chicks in pens really grated on my senses. I picked up one helpless little bundle of fluff. It gazed up at me with loving – nay – trusting eyes, as I slowly squeezed the life out of it and bit its head off. (Not.) I love animals and didn't fancy working in a place like that for long. I'd want to let them all out to make a humane break for freedom.

The fresh air outside was, well, a breath of fresh air. I decided to visit the factory and find out what they made. Having slogged my guts out for six months in an English factory to save enough money for this trip, I didn't relish the thought of having to work inside (especially when the weather was so great) – but volunteers can't be choosers.

It was very noisy, hot and smelly inside. I discovered that they made metal parts for other machines. And plastic. Ho hum. How bloody interesting. I wondered if there was another factory on the kibbutz where they made paint and then watched it dry...with over-time?

I was really hoping for a job that involved the great outdoors. It wasn't my plan to come all this way for the sun and then be stuck indoors. But I knew for a fact that every new volunteer had to start work on the dishwasher. Moreover, the other volunteers had already told me that as an initiation ritual, I had to go through the dishwasher with just my swimming shorts on.

I would find out the next morning if I had to imitate a dirty plate.

Thursday 7 May

Thank God it was a wind-up. This job was awful. If sinners had to wash endless dishes in Hell I had a good idea of what they went through. There were two busy times on the dishwasher. The first was the breakfast period from 6-8am, and then the lunch period from noon until about 2pm.

After each of these joyful periods I had to empty, drain and clean the machine until I could see my face in it. There were scraps of food stuck in every orifice. I found bent cutlery wedged in places I didn't even know existed. I had played safe and laughed in the face of fashion by wearing my free work clothes. My front was soaked with dirty dishwater, and my back with sweat from the steam. Bits of boiled chicken were hanging from my eyebrows and I had a soggy carrot protruding from my pocket.

I could see the look of relief in Ben's eyes as he walked through because I had taken his place in the dishwasher job. A quick water fight began which he lost miserably.

Beatrice plodded through and told me that I would be introduced to my kibbutz parents at the special Sabbath meal the following evening. Every volunteer was assigned an 'adoptive' family on the kibbutz, the idea being that we had a home to go to for tea, chats and family life.

Friday is the most important day of the week in Israel, as it heralds the beginning of the religious rest-day which starts at sundown on the Friday night, when the special Shabbat, or Sabbath, meal is held. The whole of Israel effectively shuts down from then until Saturday sunset. The members took it in turns to prepare and serve the Shabbat food – volunteers never had to do this duty.

It is regarded as polite for volunteers to sit with their respective families. Mette told me that I would have the same kibbutz parents as her (or KPs as she called them for short).

3pm: Finished work for the day. Most of the other volunteers were already at the accommodation blocks so we just lazed around on a climbing frame and chatted.

The kibbutz supplied us with a daily English language newspaper, The Jerusalem Post. It only consisted of twelve pages on a good day but it was better than nothing. The front page story was about a Jewish woman who had been stabbed to death by an Arab while she was shopping in Haifa. Violent attacks like this could be commonplace in Israel, but the members were still shocked by each and every one.

Friday 8 May

My first Shabbat. This was the only meal, apart from special occasions like festivals, when tablecloths were used. We would also be having wine. I wasn't really a wine lover, but any free alcohol was just fine with me. It would also be my first chance to visit the legendary boiling pot of excessive drinking and wild partying – the Naloz pub.

7pm: Dressed up to the nines (clean jeans and t-shirts), us volunteers trooped over for the Shabbat meal.

Mette introduced me to my new KPs, Assaf and Anat. They were extremely friendly and easy to get on with, but then again I hadn't met a member yet who had been anything but welcoming. As usual with most Israelis, my KPs' English was excellent. They had a young son, who I suppose was my 'adopted' brother.

When everybody was seated I realised it was the first time that I had seen every kibbutz member in the dining room at the same time. It was packed and there was a great atmosphere. Before we started to eat, a woman sang a song in Hebrew and said a short prayer. Then she said 'Shabbat Shalom' which literally means: 'Hello Shabbat'.

The food was served, heralding a horrible sight. Women were being elbowed for a piece of fried chicken; old people were prodding each other with forks for the last slurp of soup; volunteers were squeezing the wine bottles for the last drop (we knew our priorities in life). It was a meal time massacre.

10pm: Back to the volunteers' blocks for a party before the pub opened at midnight. Ben and Peter had 'borrowed' some spare wine from the meal and were busy making a punch with it, along with some vodka, rum and brandy. Plus some orange juice to keep it healthy and some bottles of beer to wash it down with.

As my vision began to blur, so Mette began to look more attractive. I took a quick imaginary cold shower, it was not a good idea for volunteers to get involved with each other – if things didn't work out it would probably get a bit uncomfortable. We lit some candles and played drinking games while The Doors sung about breaking on through to the other side. Midnight arrived – pub time!

One of the most generous/foolish policies of Kibbutz Naloz was that everything was free for members and volunteers in the pub on Friday nights. They apparently made so much money from the paying public on Saturdays that they could easily afford it.

Who were we to complain? Besides, at that point we could hardly walk or talk. Still we made it. The pub was divided into a bar area and a dance floor with seating around the edge. The place was large enough to hold everybody, but still had an intimate feel to it. The dance floor was bordered with large mirrors on the wall, which came in handy, as one of the passions of the Israelis (and I say this in the nicest way) is to constantly check their appearance as they make their 'Mick Jagger moves'. But really, nobody in that seething mass of disco mania really gave a shit: they were just enjoying themselves.

I joined Ben and Peter at the bar and we had some Tequila Slammers. At one point we substituted the lemonade for vodka and were so pissed that we couldn't work out why our 'Slammers' didn't fizz up when banged on the bar – these South Africans really knew how to drink. A few moments later they really knew how to fall off their stools. I had originally hoped to get to know some of the Israeli girls that night. All I hoped for by the end of the night was that my body's automatic pilot system would be able to locate my bed.

Saturday 9 May

Day off. I awoke and hoped that I hadn't made a fool of myself on my first night at the pub. There seemed to be a heavy metal band living in my head and my stomach was gurgling like a drain. I resolved never to drink again. Or until that night anyway.

I dragged myself over to the dining room to meet the other volunteers. We all sat at the same table and it soon became apparent that this particular meal always served as a 'post mortem' of events that might have happened the night before.

Dorte told us that Mette hadn't come back to her room and had been seen leaving the pub with Peter. That neither of them had been sighted as yet, seemed to confirm this piece of gossip. One main feature of any kibbutz is that everybody knows everything about everyone else – there is no privacy whatsoever. So if a person became involved in any scandal or gossip, it would be common knowledge by the next day.

Beer and Bagels for Breakfast

We were stuck on the kibbutz on Saturdays because no buses ran on Shabbat. I went back to my room and crashed out for the afternoon to 'Wish You Were Here' by Pink Floyd.

8pm: Laundry time. Linda told me that clothes sometimes went missing because people had forgotten to mark them with their names. It would be easy to spot one of my t-shirts being worn by someone else – but I didn't have much chance if a pair of boxer shorts went walkies! Clean sheets were given out every Saturday and this was also the place to order extra work clothes or boots.

I got chatting to a member called Dana who worked in the laundry. She was twenty years old and had recently finished her army service. She explained to me that in Israel, boys had to serve three years in the army when they turned eighteen, and girls had to serve for two. I felt myself being drawn into her large brown eyes as she spoke about tanks and guns in her sexy accent. My own barrel felt like it was fully loaded and ready to fire. I arranged to meet Dana later that night in the pub. Yes!

10.30pm: The pub opened earlier on Saturday nights to cater for the public. I walked in and couldn't believe how popular it was. Jenny told me that this was because the only other entertainment around the area was a town about five miles away called Stirot. Other local kibbutzim had their own pubs as well, but the one on Naloz was apparently the best. It began to look like I had struck it lucky by coming here.

I saw Dana by the bar and she introduced me to her group of friends, including Avatel, whom Ben was seeing. The beers had to be paid for on Saturday nights and cost two shekels each for people living on Naloz. When the pub closed at 4am, I walked Dana to her room and then went back to the volunteers' blocks. I fondly remembered how her tongue had played sweet music on my tonsil piano.

Sunday 10 May

I thought that today was meant to be a day of rest, but evidently not in Israel. Working on a Sunday would definitely take some getting used to. I had my AIDS test this afternoon. I've always been able to handle needles, but not the sight of blood coming out of one of my own veins. Results back next week.

Monday 11 May

9pm: We heard that there would be a party tonight on Kibbutz Gerim, about thirty minutes walk away from Naloz. Even though we had not been invited we decided to embark on a volunteer mission to 'go in, get the job done and get out' in true SAS style.

Our raiding group included Ben, Peter, Anne, Jenny, Linda and myself. Mette and Dorte decided to stay back and wash their hair, (including the tresses under their armpits).

We reached Gerim and soon located the party, which was being held underground in one of their bomb shelters. Every kibbutz has a few bomb shelters; most in the safer areas of the country are used for storage, but in the north it's another story. We stood outside and listened to a Clash song pumping up the stairs. I heard the singer: '...should I stay or should I go now...?' and asked myself the same question, as their members might not have taken kindly to some uninvited guests turning up. Brave Liverpudlian Linda made the decision for us and went down the steps. The shelter was hot and smoky and the music very loud in such a confined space. A large Israeli lumbered over and asked us who we were. Ben said that we were new volunteers who had just arrived on a late bus. The ploy worked and the Gerim member told us what we wanted to hear: 'OK – grab a beer.'

We found some of the Gerim volunteers whom we knew from attending the Naloz pub, and they said that they wouldn't give the game away. Party on dudes!

11pm: Totally pissed and giving each other piggy-backs to Kibbutz Naloz we had one of those great ideas that people only seem to have when the worse for drink. Why don't we put a cow in the dining room to greet the members at breakfast time? The girls saw sense and went to bed with shouts of: 'stupid bastards!'

Peter, Ben and myself managed to locate the cow sheds more through luck (and smell) than anything else. We spied our 'guest', cow number 294, watching us warily from the other side of the shed.

Shushing and cursing each other much too loudly, we began to negotiate our way through the mud over to her. It smelt really weird. Of course, reader. It was shit.

Ben shouted out as he fell over on hands and knees. I slipped over and Peter was already sitting in it.

It's amazing how quick one sobers up when one realises that one is caked in crap.

Cow number 294 mocked us with a flick of her ears as we slid back to the volunteers' blocks.

Wednesday 13 May

Visited the kibbutz shop with Dana. She invited me over to her room later that night and we bought some nibbles and a bottle of wine. I stocked up on hangover tablets and noticed that condoms were free.

The shop was not extravagant but contained most things that people needed from day to day like cigarettes, groceries, drinks and toiletries.

Cards were credited with the wages that the kibbutz gave us. We could take the money off the card or add to it like a bank account. A little credit is normally given, but I had changed some traveller's cheques up in the kibbutz office and added four hundred shekels to my account. For larger items or for a better choice of clothes, it was best to go into Tel Aviv. Members received free bus passes from the kibbutz but volunteers didn't, which was a shame as it would have been a useful perk for us.

I spent a fun night round at Dana's. We strengthened our relationship with a delicate balance of exquisite conversation, fragile sensitivity and a thumping good shag.

Thursday 14 May

My red skin was finally turning into a golden brown colour. Anne took a photo of me to send home to my family to prove that I could look healthy now and again.

Friday 15 May

A new volunteer arrived – Einar from Norway. He was going to share my room and Beatrice arranged to move another bed in there. Einar told me that he was recovering from a nervous breakdown and had come to Israel to: '...get my head together'. So it seemed that my roommate was either going to turn out to be a manic-depressive or a psycho. Great choice.

After work, I took Einar on a guided tour of the kibbutz. It was surprising how quickly the layout could be learnt, especially when living, working and eating in the same place for twenty-four hours a day, but I remembered how daunting it had seemed when I first arrived. The arrival of a new volunteer meant that I could leave the dishwasher. I planned to check out my new job the following day when the work list was posted up on the dining room notice board.

In the evening the volunteers had a welcoming piss-up for Einar but he didn't really seem interested in joining in.

Saturday 16 May

I felt really great in the morning – Dana and myself were getting along like a house on fire. My head was clear and the world was a bowl of peaches!

The post mortem during lunch revealed that Peter and Mette were seeing each other. The word had soon spread along the kibbutz grapevine and Jewish tongues were wagging ten-to-the-dozen. Why did I feel that being a volunteer was like living in a goldfish bowl?

I checked the work list and discovered that I would be working with the cows, which meant a 4am start – I could barely wait.

I went for an afternoon walk with Dana to the fields. We took some cold beers and sandwiches and just relaxed. I wondered what the winter would be like in Israel. Considering the fact that the area we were in was technically a desert, I bet it would be freezing.

11pm: Persuaded Einar to check out the pub. He seemed to loosen up a tad. Actually, I think that Linda took a shine to him.

Sunday 17 May

10am: Finished my shift with the cows. I went straight there from the pub as it wasn't worth going to bed. The job wasn't too bad. It was an early start but at least I finished with most of the day free. I did wonder if I could request a later shift on Saturday mornings, otherwise my social life would seriously suffer. My job was to attach the milking machine to the cows after they had been herded through the dairy. It took about four hours to finish the whole herd and then we had to hose the floors down and clean and sterilise the machinery. It was the first time in my life that I'd had a cup of tea where the milk was squirted in straight from the cow! I hoped it was healthy – did they have 'mad cow disease' in Israel?

Monday 18 May

Got my AIDS test back. 'It's negative,' Beatrice said matter-of-factly. I could have kissed her (but resisted the urge). Not for one moment did I think that it would be positive. But it was the first AIDS test I'd had in my life and the nagging question had been playing in the back of my mind.

Tuesday 19 May

Two weeks since I arrived – time has flown. I had met a lot of members, and realised that if I made an effort to get to know the Israelis they would do the same in return.

Wednesday 20 May

It's tricky stomaching salad for breakfast every day. The only other choices were toast, cereal that tasted like cardboard, cream cheese and yoghurt or hard-boiled eggs.

I would have sold my grandmother for a plate of greasy sausages, bacon, fried eggs, mushrooms and baked beans drowned in tomato sauce and washed down with a glass of fresh orange juice, but I don't think the bacon would have gone down too well in kosher Israel.

I could feel my stomach shrinking as I munched another carrot; at least my eyesight was improving.

Thursday 21 May

A poignant day. Anne, the first person who had welcomed me into the bosom of the volunteer family, told me she was leaving on Friday to travel around the country, so that left eight volunteers including myself.

We decided to throw a surprise leaving party for her. Jenny and Linda made a cake, whilst Mette and Dorte designed a leaving card. Ben, Peter and yours truly purchased some refreshments from the shop. Einar just gazed vacantly into space. Beatrice made a guest appearance at the party and thanked Anne for her hard work. She gave her a bar of chocolate as a leaving present and told her not to eat it all at once.

Friday 22 May

Received a letter from England. It was from my family just making sure that they had the right address...and was I really so near to Gaza?

9pm: Visited my KPs and found out my kibbutz 'uncle' Dov, was also the work manager for the volunteers. That's handy Harry! I decided to look out for a job with better hours. Skipped the pub for the first time since I'd arrived on the kibbutz and spent a cosy night with Dana.

Saturday 23 May

We were told the swimming pool would be opening on June 1 and were asked to help to clean it in our spare time. You bet your last goddamm shekel we could!

It was a great laugh. Most of the kibbutz youth were helping and water fights were the order of the day. We literally had to get on our hands and knees and scrub every inch of the pool with scouring pads. It would be worth it though – the weather was definitely hot enough for us to swim now.

Sunday 24 May

5am: Sore head from drinking. Sewer stomach. Smell of cow shit. Decided I would request a new job later that day.

2pm: Went to have a quiet word with Dov, and asked if I could be moved from the cows to something else. I told him the hours were insane and I thought cow number 391 had been eyeing me up in a most flirtatious way. Dov said that I would have to stay there until another volunteer arrived to take my place.

I had a shower and went over to Dana's to watch MTV.

In the evening the volunteers had a pool tournament in the games room. The pool table wasn't perfect; it's the only table I've ever played on that enabled me to pot balls around corners – but it was free. Felt a bit pissed off at not being able to switch jobs so I went to bed and hoped that another volunteer would soon turn up to take my place in the cows.

Monday 25 May

I did something that was truly special today – I helped a cow to give birth! We were having a tea break at about 7.30am, when we were told to go to the shed where the pregnant cows were kept apart from the others. Uri was already in there, standing by a cow that had a spindly pair of legs hanging out from where the sun don't shine. He said that the cow was having some difficulty in giving birth, and he tied a rope around the calf's legs and told me to pull. I was very apprehensive and the grunts of the cow didn't help much to steady my nerves. So I pulled back and thought of England.

There was a squelching noise and the calf slid out quicker than I could say 'milkshake'. It definitely had its mother's eyes.

Tuesday 26 May

Day off because it was Shavuot (Feast of Weeks). This is an agri-cultural festival marking the wheat harvest. All the kibbutz members went out to the fields, where they had set up stalls and a little zoo, which had rabbits, goats and guinea pigs for the kibbutz children to look after. A group of soldiers had arrived and were walking around brandishing their rifles. This was in case any Arabs decided to gatecrash the festival and cause trouble. The Israelis didn't take any chances as far as their security was concerned.

Everybody stood and watched as a combine harvester went into the field and symbolically cut the first of the wheat. After the harvest ceremony, a special dinner was served, similar to a Friday night and I sat with Dana and her family.

Before the meal some of the members stood on a little stage and sang some songs. I didn't have the faintest idea what they were going on about but clapped along with everyone else. I decided to make an effort to pick up some Hebrew lingo from then on.

So far all I knew was 'benzona' which roughly translated means: 'You're a pubic hair on the toilet seat of humanity'. I wouldn't get far with that.

Wednesday 27 May

I took a day off and went into Stirot (a nearby town) with Dana.
Stirot was very small but had a few useful shops. There was a
bank, a pizza parlour, a hairdresser, a few tiny bars, a cinema and
two – yes TWO – nightclubs. Dana told me The Warehouse was open
on Friday and Saturday nights, but The Shooting Star was only open
on a Saturday because the owner was religious and wouldn't open
the club on Shabbat.

We both had a pizza and then went for some beers at a bar and
I signed a book that other visiting volunteers from the past had put
their names in. It went as far back as 1982. I was honoured to be
listed next to such literary greats as 'Colin Woz 'Ere', 'Sarah's a
SLAG!' and 'Tottenham Forever!'

Thursday 28 May

Small drama when a cow escaped and ran amok. The fugitive
tried to make a break for it through the fence. Big mistake. Caught
in the electrified wire, it looked like it was auditioning for a break-
dancing competition. Luckily its own body weight pulled it free. It
just stood there stunned. Ever seen a cow looking sheepish?

Friday 29 May

Two new Brazilian volunteers arrived on Naloz. The guy's name
was Arthur (pronounced Ar-tor) and his girlfriend's name was
Margarite. Kibbutz policy was to give couples their own room. The
arrival of Arthur meant that I could make my escape from the dairy.
I had a chat with Dov and told him that I wanted an outside job. It
was best to lay it on thick with the Israelis and not to beat around
the bush. I hinted: 'Put me to work ploughing the land, sowing the
seed and reaping the golden harvest.'

Dov offered me a factory position.

I offered to spread vicious rumours about him, female underwear and a goat with no name.

He told me that there was no vacancy in the fields, but would I
like to try my hand at being a kibbutz gardener? Does a bear shit in
the woods Dov?

9pm: The volunteers held a welcoming party for Arthur and

Margarite. They had brought a tape of Brazilian folk music with them. We made a bonfire outside the volunteers' blocks and lazed around it with beers and vodka, whilst the Brazilian drums beat a steady rhythm in time with the crickets.

I felt a bit horny, so slipped away to meet Dana before the pub opened.

The pub was fantastic – some of the members whose family roots were in Morocco organised a party. There was spicy Moroccan food laid out on tables and mats had been put on the floor for us to lounge on. We sipped cocktails, listened to ethnic Moroccan music and lost ourselves in the atmosphere. The highlight was a display by a belly dancer. It was a mesmerising show, but I assured Dana that I only had eyes for her.

The pub was packed and all the members were clapping and singing. I looked around and saw that all ten volunteers were joining in the festivities.

Einar had managed to grab a front row seat and his eyes were bulging out like a frog's. Mette and Dorte were dancing in the corner and imitating the belly dancer's movements. Ben and Peter were pissed as farts and shouting: 'Tits out for the Afrikaaners!'

Sexist bastards I thought... and glued my eyes back onto the half-naked dancer's luscious womanly curves.

Saturday 30 May

I had a hangover the size of Israel's defence budget – massive!

After some volunteer gossip at lunch it emerged that Einar and Linda had felt the earth move together the previous night. This occurred when Einar had fallen on Linda whilst in a drunken stupor and knocked her out. I still hoped that those two would get it together at some stage. Einar had mumbled Linda's name in his sleep a few times over the past week. He must have fancied her. Either that, or she was his worst nightmare. I decided to play matchmaker.

2pm: We played a game of softball on the football field. It was the Volunteer All Stars against ten of the Israelis. The other team had played softball many times before and thrashed us. Their team was over the moon but I felt as sick as a parrot. Every man gave one hundred and ten percent but our star player was Arthur. The lad did good.

10.30pm: I went to the pub in the evening and it was heaving. It was easy to make sure that Einar and Linda would attend and manoeuvre them onto the same table. Then I threw the cat among the chickens and told each one separately that they fancied the other. Jenny called me a stirrer.

We now had to wait and let nature take its course. Talking of nature, my new gardening job started the following day. Raring to grow.

Sunday 31 May

My new hours were generally 8am to 2pm.

I had a lettuce sandwich (yuck!) for breakfast and went to the gardening headquarters, the Noy.

Dan, my new boss, was aged about sixty. A few members had warned me that he was one of the hardest-working men on the whole kibbutz. His Hebrew nickname meant 'wire'; apparently he could make anything out of anything.

Dan said that I could be guaranteed a job in the Noy for the rest of my year on Naloz if I worked hard.

My first task was to study a plan of the kibbutz and learn the layout of the lawns, sprinkler systems, certain types of plants and so on.

Dan informed me that he would tell me what my day's work was to be and then trust me to get on with it unsupervised. There was only the two of us working in the Noy at the time, but if I needed Dan for anything, he could always be found in the grounds somewhere.

I cut the grass around the swimming pool in preparation for its opening the following day.

3pm: Finished work. Dan said the hours were flexible and some days I would finish earlier or later than expected.

Beer and Bagels for Breakfast

JUNE

Monday 1 June

I drove a tractor for the first time in my life. Dan told me to drive around the kibbutz and collect any rubbish or dead branches that were blocking the pathways. Whilst chugging around, I bumped into a lot of my friends, and when I stopped by the children's nursery to cut down an old bush, the woman in charge invited me in for coke and a cake.

I sped by the dairy and stuck my fingers up at Arthur. He was waiting in ambush and soaked me with a hose as I drove by. The weather was really hot now and I was soon dry. I then drove out to the fields to dump the rubbish in the pit. The tricky part was reversing the trailer as close to the edge of the pit as possible without sliding in backwards; there was a gradual slope leading into the pit, which was covered with old food from the kitchens, and it looked too slippery to come back up again.

The members dumped all kinds of things in there: oil drums, plastic bags, gardening waste – and even a dead cow. Its legs were sticking straight out of the water at the bottom of the pit and reminded me of a swallow dive that had gone wrong. There was a cute little bird balancing on one of its hoofs and singing a sweet melody. It brought a lump to my throat.

I swallowed my breakfast back down (the smell was disgusting out there) and drove back to the kibbutz.

Some Arabs were working in the fields, employed by the kibbutz as cheap labour.

There were a lot of random attacks happening to Jews across the country. Touched with paranoia, I thought that if an Arab threw a wobbly, how would he know I wasn't a Jew?

1pm: I finished work early and joined the volunteers at the busy swimming pool. Music from a radio station pumped out from a couple of loudspeakers by the tea and coffee area. Peter, Ben and Arthur were 'bombing' each other and got a warning from the lifeguard to stop. Einar was chatting to Linda and finally seemed to be coming out of his shell.

Mette, Dorte, Jenny and Margarite were soaking up some serious rays. Peter pushed me in the pool so I sat on the bottom for a bit to make him think I was drowning. It was about four metres deep at the end and very quiet down there. Being a typical Piscean I felt quite at home.

Beer and Bagels for Breakfast

My mind drifted to what my family would be doing back in England. I thought of them struggling to get out of bed on a rainy Monday morning (if it was a normal English summer) and going to work. When I'd left for Israel I thought that a one-year stay might be too long. Now, I had a sneaking feeling that it would be over too soon.

Tuesday 2 June

The Palestinians were up to mischief this morning. There was a huge column of black smoke winding its way up from Gaza City and it was clearly visible from the kibbutz. I drove the tractor to the volunteers' blocks and grabbed my camera to take a photo.

Wednesday 3 June

Einar took a trip into the Twilight Zone.
As it was getting dark, he crept over to the chicken sheds and killed a chicken by twisting its neck. He brought the body back to the volunteers' rooms and plucked all the feathers out. Then he took it into our washroom and gutted it. There was blood splashed over the sink and some had spilled onto the floor. Talk about a gruesome sight. But worse was to come.
Einar then made a little bonfire, cooked some of the chicken and ate it. This was 'Lord of the Flies'.
I couldn't believe that he had done this and asked him why. He said: 'Because it was the purest meal that I've ever eaten.'
When the other volunteers found out what he had done they were disgusted. Even Linda, who thought the sun shone out of his arse. I went to see Dana but never mentioned anything about what Einar had done. If the kibbutz members found out they had a serial chicken killer within their midst then there would be trouble. It hit me then, how the volunteers could cover up for each other. I suppose that I was just looking after number one, in a way, because I didn't want the kibbutz community to think that all the volunteers could do sick things like that.
But I wasn't too happy about sharing a room with Einar after that.

Thursday 4 June

At work I went on a killing spree myself. My job was to walk around the kibbutz with a spray machine on my back eliminating weeds. When the tank was full with chemicals it was bloody heavy and the straps cut into my shoulder blades. But, like the trooper I am, there was to be no flinching from my duty.

Friday 5 June

After work there was a football match between the members and volunteers in mixed teams. There wasn't much skill shown but a lot of enthusiasm.

I'm not very good at football and would much rather have been in the swimming pool but didn't want to let the side down. The members seem to think that every Englishman has a golden boot. In my case it's two left feet. I was sweating like a pig and very tired from my morning's work, which had involved carrying heavy irrigation pipes around with Dan.

10pm: The volunteers played a drinking game involving obscene amounts of alcohol, spinning wine bottles and doing dares. It was a pitiful sight watching Arthur performing a naked handstand out on the lawn.

11pm: They played some excellent music in the pub – people were really raving and must have drunk the place dry. I asked the bloke who ran the pub if I could have a go at being DJ and he said I could do it some time.

Saturday 6 June

Ben walked into lunch minus one eyebrow. Peter had shaved it off while he was in a drunken stupor. I hoped that his actions weren't going to start an eyebrow war; I was quite attached to mine.

In the afternoon, we had permission to take one of the tractors out to the fields for a picnic. Some of the kibbutz kids came with us and we had a relaxed time.

4pm: Just time to have a muck around in the pool for a couple of hours. I'd decided that it would be a good idea to try and organise a pool party for the middle of the week. The other volunteers were keen on the idea.

Beer and Bagels for Breakfast

8pm: Took my dirty laundry over and invited Dana to Stirot with us. She said that she would give it a miss as she felt like an early night.

10pm: Volunteers were not allowed to borrow the kibbutz cars so we had to arrange a lift into town.

It was ten shekels to get into The Shooting Star, which included one free beer. The music was mainly techno, rave and disco but the odd rock track was played. Beers were six shekels a bottle.

After a couple of hours we decided to try out The Warehouse.

I thought that the second club was much better. It was free to get in and beers were also six shekels. As the name suggests, this place was set out in the style of a warehouse and had a more intense, earthy feel to it. The music played was the same as in The Shooting Star, but this place was packed with young Israelis and volunteers from other local kibbutzim in the area.

The music, heat and intimate atmosphere went to my head and I got off with an Israeli girl who was flirting with me. I felt very guilty thinking about Dana back at the kibbutz but my flesh was weak.

When the club shut, our group of volunteers managed to hitch a lift back to Naloz on the back of a vegetable truck. Ben and Peter were throwing potatoes at passing cars; Linda was trying to keep her balance on a sack of carrots and Jenny was comparing a cucumber to a past boyfriend's anatomy.

Sunday 7 June

A shitty day. Dana found out about me sharing tongue sarnies with another girl. One of her friends must have been in The Warehouse and saw what was going on. I had no excuse and felt like a total bastard.

Dana asked me to go and see her after work. She called me a 'nudnik' which means 'waste of space', and said that it was over; finished; kaput. How could I have been so stupid?

It was time to hit the cheap Israeli brandy and listen to 'Dark Side of the Moon'.

Monday 8 June

2am: Woke up in a cold sweat. I dreamt that I was buried up to my neck in the middle of a large lawn. I could see a herd of cows thundering towards me from the other end of the field but I was trapped and couldn't move my head. They were all twitching around as though a giant puppeteer was jerking their strings up and down. I couldn't even scream for help because I had a massive lettuce sandwich wedged into my mouth.

If that wasn't bad enough, there was also a scrawny chicken pecking the wax out of my ears.

Suddenly I heard a loud mechanical buzzing sound approaching from behind. Even though I couldn't turn my head to look, I just knew that it was a Lawnmower From Hell bearing down to give me rather more than a short back and sides.

I could hear Einar's voice moaning from the cows' mouths: 'We're doomed...we're dooooomed!'

Just as the whirr of the blades shaved the back of my neck, I managed to wake up shouting: 'I am not a blade of grass! I'm a free man!'

I looked over at Einar's huddled shape on the other side of the room. He hadn't stirred.

Tuesday 9 June

I popped over to the laundry to see Dana, but she didn't want to know. I was learning fast that Israeli girls place loyalty high on their list of priorities.

Thursday 11 June

Depression lifting. The sun was shining and the birds were singing.

There was now a lot of hard physical work to be done in the Noy. Dan and I had to repair some of the lawn sprinklers. I could see how Dan had earned his reputation as a hard worker; despite being at an age when most English pensioners are planning their retirement, he could wield a shovel with the best of 'em.

He told me that he had joined the kibbutz in his twenties and could remember running from flying bullets across the fields – and there I was worrying about getting a sunburnt nose.

He was a typical kibbutznik who loved his way of life and keeping the kibbutz in a condition to be proud of; Dan's enthusiasm couldn't help but influence me to do a good job. It felt great to be working with water on such a hot day, as the heat in Israel is a very dry heat – not humid as it is in England. I was really brown by now and feeling much fitter than I had done for ages.

I presumed it must be the healthy food, regular exercise and peace of mind. Everything is laid on for people who live on a kibbutz with no worries about mortgages or where the next meal is coming from.

1pm: Beatrice called a volunteer meeting after lunch and told us that we were all going on a volunteer trip the following Wednesday to the Kinneret (Sea of Galilee).

Things really were picking up.

Friday 12 June

Work was great fun today. Dan and I had to burn off some grassy areas around the outskirts of the kibbutz. As yours truly is a pyro-maniac, it was a dream come true. We hitched up a large water tank to the back of the tractor in case the fires started to spread. Our only defence against the raging inferno was a tool that resembled a rubber oar to beat out the smaller blazes.

We had a supply of old newspapers and Dan lit one and threw it into a large clump of dead brown bushes. The middle started to burn immediately, and before I could say 'amazing arsonists' the fire was off and running. So were we.

Dan started to babble on in Hebrew and gestured for me to get around the other side of the flames. I had to beat out tiny rogue fires and concentrate on guiding the main one into the right areas that had to be cleared. The heat was intense and my bare legs, arms and face had black streaks on them from the smoke and charcoal. One side of the wasteland that we were burning was lined with trees, and a few of these caught the flames and started to go up as well, shooting glowing cinders into the air. Dan got the tractor engine running and the attached water pump started to douse and contain the edges of the fire. I connected another hose to an irriga-tion pipe set in the ground and went around to the far side of the fire to dampen it down. I had heard of the 'Burning Bush' but never thought that I would actually start one!

There were small animals running out of the undergrowth to safety and birds were circling and tweeting for the others to follow them. Smoke was everywhere and my eyes watered constantly, but we eventually got the fire under control. We would leave the area to cool for a day or so, and then plough it for future agricultural use.

5pm: Finished work slightly later because we had to be sure that all the fires were completely out. It wouldn't be on to be accepted into the hospitality of Kibbutz Naloz only to raze it to the ground.

11pm: My body was begging for beer. I must have lost more fluid than I thought whilst running around and beating out the fire earlier. I felt too drained to dance, so just sat in the pub and had a few scoops of ale.

Saturday 13 June

Ben, Peter, Arthur and myself played the war game 'Risk' on the lawn before lunch. As our troops engaged in bloody battle on the board, we drank a few beers and chatted about life in general.

Arthur confided in us that his girl, Margarite, wanted to go back to Brazil but he wanted to stay on the kibbutz. He said: 'I've seen so many beautiful girls in Israel that now the ugly ones look interesting.'

Ben muttered: 'Well Arthur... if you want to visit a restaurant don't take a packed lunch along mate.'

Peter took a sip of his beer, threw a double six and conquered Europe in one fell swoop.

8pm: Took my dirty sheets to the laundry and saw Dana there. I felt that it was up to me to try and break the Israeli ice so I asked her if she could help me look for my lost sock. It was the only pathetic thing that sprang to mind. At least we were talking, and she agreed to let me buy her a drink later in the pub. I could see that she was going to make it hard for me.

11pm: Met Dana and some of her mates. Damn it – if I was going to have to profusely grovel then I'd hoped it was going to be in private. I started to apologise for being a complete prat, but it's quite difficult to whisper sweet nothings to the girl you fancy while 'James Brown Is Dead' thumps out of loudspeakers about a foot away from your head. Dana shouted something to her mate in Hebrew and started laughing. Then she took my hand and dragged me into the sea of bodies on the dance floor. It seemed that all was forgiven...

Later, we continued dancing the night away – horizontally.

Beer and Bagels for Breakfast

Sunday 14 June

5.50am: Rolled out of Dana's bed, went back to my room to put some work clothes on, and got to the Noy with minutes to spare.

Dan was already there and busy fixing the plough to the back of the tractor. Apparently, the waste ground that we'd cleared was now cool enough to be turned over. Dan drove up and down a few times to give me a demonstration of how it was done. If the wheels got stuck in the soil, a lever was pulled and the plough automatically lifted up at the back so that the tractor could pull itself free. Easy...

Climbing into the driver's seat, I engaged first gear, lowered the plough and churned off towards the other end of the field.

Everything went fine for the first ten minutes. That was until I saw the tree stump protruding from the earth in my path.

My life flashed before my eyes...leaving a dark tunnel...my first birthday...Andy Pandy books...Slade on Top of the Pops...fumbling with a girl's bra strap...

The front wheel hit the stump and the tractor bounced up into the air. I bounced up in my seat and landed heavily on a testicle. The worst pain known to man flashed through my stomach. I yelled something like: 'Make love in Satan's home'.

The plough snagged the tree stump, there was a jerking movement and it sheared off from the tractor with a loud cracking noise. Then everything stopped. The engine cut out and a tranquil silence descended upon God's good Earth. I sat there for some time while my throbbing bollock recovered, before hobbling off to find Dan.

Reluctantly I told him what had happened, but he just laughed and told me that sort of accident happened a lot on the kibbutz – it wasn't the first time and it wouldn't be the last. We went back to the Noy, got some nuts and bolts and returned to the tractor.

Dan cut the broken part off with a hacksaw and bolted the plough back onto the tractor quicker than two shakes of a spanner. Now I understood why his nickname was 'wire'.

Monday 15 June

Margarite left for Brazil, but Arthur decided to stay. She left on amicable terms and said that she would meet up with him when he returned home. It was a very strange time to leave just before a free trip, but she said that kibbutz life didn't really appeal to her. Fair enough – you either love it or hate it. So that left nine volunteers on Kibbutz Naloz: me, Ben, Peter, Mette, Dorte, Jenny, Linda, Arthur and good old Einar. I thought it was a good-sized group, because we could all get to know each other well. I knew of one large kibbutz where there could be anything up to one hundred and twenty volunteers. Because of the large numbers they were treated like cattle.

Tuesday 16 June

2pm: I finished work and went to the kitchens to prepare some food for the trip the following day.

We would be sleeping under the stars and cooking our own food. Items packed included sleeping bags, a cooking stove, pots, tinned food, bread, eggs, a drinks cooler, two boxes of beer and – of course – a bottle opener. Apart from the volunteers, Beatrice was going with us and Guy, the kibbutz cook, would be our driver. He was about fifty, very gruff but a good laugh.

I thought of Dana – three whole days away from my kibbutz cutie. I flipped a shekel: Heads – absence makes the heart grow fonder; Tails – out of sight out of mind.

It spun through the air in slow motion, glinting in the golden rays of the sun and started to float downwards...

With a grin Beatrice caught it and put it in her pocket.

7pm: Skipped dinner (I couldn't handle toast and soup) and went to Dana's for a goodbye cuddle.

Roll on the Sea of Galilee.

Wednesday 17 June

We had breakfast, put our travel bags into the minibus and set off just after 8am. The sun was shining and it was a glorious day. We had shades on our eyes, beers in our hands and Lenny Kravitz in our ears. The open road lay ahead.

Our planned route took us up along the West coast of Israel as far as Hadera and then north-east to Tiberias – a town on the shores of the Kinneret.

The journey took roughly four hours, so we chatted and joked around a bit. Even Beatrice seemed in a holiday mood, which wasn't surprising really as she was enjoying time off work as well.

Beer and Bagels for Breakfast

Guy drove the minibus and occasionally changed the tapes while he told us amusing stories about his early life on Kibbutz Naloz. It sounded as though he'd been a bit of a lad in his time. During relaxed times such as these, it was easy to forget that I was in a country that was still technically at war with others.

1pm: Arrived at a camping ground situated on the shores of the Sea of Galilee. Well it's a lake really but absolutely massive. Beatrice told us that it's the main water supply for the country and at that moment it seemed quite full.

We wasted no time in changing into our swimming gear and taking the plunge. Well, if Jesus could walk on it then I was sure as hell going to swim in it!

It was very warm and just like swimming in a sea without the salt. While we all splashed around and ducked each other, Guy and Beatrice started to prepare lunch. It was very advantageous having a cook as our driver. Later, we all helped to cook dinner on an open fire. I was in charge of the chips but screwed them up and they turned out soggy. There was salad, steaks and a plentiful supply of cold beers.

After dinner, the volunteers headed into the town of Tiberias to check it out. It was quite disappointing in that it catered for the tourist that had just come to view the Sea. We made base in a friendly pub and stayed there for the rest of the evening.

Thursday 18 June

2am: We were woken up by the sound of a helicopter flying very close to the water. Its searchlight was on and pointing downwards.

A large fire could be seen spreading through trees up in the hills near to the camp. The flames looked like a stream of red lava as they moved very slowly down the hillsides. As we watched, the helicopter collected water in a large container suspended beneath it and flew up into the hills. When it was hovering above the fire it released the water onto the flames and extinguished some of them. Then it flew back down to the sea and repeated the exercise. This was great entertainment for us spectators but it meant that sleep was out of the question for the time being.

11am: Crawled out of my sleeping bag and evicted a fly from my nostril. Took a quick dip to wake up and joined the other volunteers for a bite to eat. Today's destination was the River Jordan.

We left the Sea of Galilee and reached our chosen spot on the river a few hours later. Guy parked the minibus and we walked to where we could hire large rubber rings. Beatrice told us these would be our transport for a few miles down the river. We all jumped in our rings and started to bob down the River Jordan. It was quite slow going at first but soon picked up through some rapids. Jenny and Linda were screaming behind me and Ben flipped over just in front. Arthur was way ahead in the 'race' but I had no idea where Einar was. Mette and Dorte held hands and squealed in Swedish while Peter and Guy spun around by the bank. Suddenly Beatrice shouted out and pointed forwards...

Just ahead of us a water snake crossed leisurely from one side to the other with its head sticking out. This didn't make me feel too happy as our arses and feet were dangling in the water. I dreaded to think what could be swimming around underneath us looking for a warm place to nest. The next stop on the tour was a nature reserve, where we went on a long signposted walk, which seemed to last forever. We saw some fascinating plants, meandering streams and old quarries and rock formations. There were good photo opportunities as well: Linda hanging upside down from a branch with her head in a stream; Ben and Peter mooning from some bushes; Einar squashing a lizard.

6pm: Reached camping ground number two and spread our sleeping bags out over the floor. We made a fire and cooked dinner. Again it was steak and chips – the same as last night, but a welcome change from kibbutz salad.

Friday 19 June

The last day of our volunteer trip had arrived too soon.

We packed our things in the minibus and headed off to the Golan Heights, the area that has contributed to most of Israel's land disputes. The rugged beauty and sweeping vistas impressed me deeply, and I could see why Israel was reluctant to give them up to Syria. We then continued close to the Lebanese border and could clearly see an army presence not far off. It was amazing to see this sort of thing with my own eyes and not through the television or through a news correspondent's words. Finally, we stopped at a park which reminded me of those back at home in England. It had a swimming pool fed by a natural spring in the hills. It was absolutely freezing! My gonads muttered 'You must be joking!' and retreated into my stomach. We could only stand about thirty minutes before giving up.

Then it was time to finish off the last of the beers as we made haste for Kibbutz Naloz. Guy drove like a man possessed and we made it back in time for the Friday night pub. Weary as we all were, it was a scorching night in there and a great end to a brilliant trip.

Saturday 20 June

Dov came over to me during lunch and said that I would have to work in the chickens the following Monday. I had to be at the chicken sheds at 10pm to work through the night but would have a day off on Tuesday to make up for it. He added that he'd already cleared it with Dan whilst I'd been on the trip.

After lunch the volunteers played softball against some of the members and we managed to beat them. Our team was definitely improving. When the game had finished we crashed out at the swimming pool and joined in a game of 'no-rules water basketball'. Someone had erected a small basketball net at the side of the pool in the shallow end. The game consisted of two teams of ten players and was quite violent but great fun.

I got out and flopped on the grass next to Dana. She teased me about how us English worship the sun. Mad dogs and volunteers...

11pm: It was getting very hot and sweaty in the pub these days because of the warm evenings and the number of people that turned up on a Saturday night in Naloz. I discovered the other volunteers at various stages of intoxication. Arthur was over in a corner chatting up a girl who worked in the kibbutz kitchens. He hadn't wasted much time since Margarite had gone home.

Einar was actually dancing for once. I could sense he was as pissed as a fart by the way he was stumbling around to 'Rhythm is a Dancer' and colliding with Mette and Dorte. They weren't too impressed by his display. Nor were the two rather large Israeli blokes that the Swedish girls were flirting with. I got the feeling that things might quickly take a turn for the worst so I sought out Ben and Peter who were propping up the bar.

They said that they would keep a (bloodshot) eye on Einar and make sure that he didn't end up as a punchbag. That was good enough for me. I went and joined Dana. Nibbling her ear, I asked if she wanted to go outside and get some fresh air, which she agreed to. The drink and few days apart had left us feeling horny. Dana suggested a midnight swim.

I had Mr Reasonable on my shoulder shouting: 'No! You're drunk! You might drown!' and Mr Hard On whispering: 'So what! Die happy!'

Mr Hard On won the argument and we followed the moonlight to the swimming pool, where I helped Dana over the fence before following her. The only sounds were the insects and the disco music thumping from yonder pub. Dana and I smooched, while the gentle breeze caused ripples to spread across the dark water. My jeans were starting to get tighter, so I decided to cool off and did a back somersault fully clothed into the pool.

It felt so refreshing and Dana dived in after me. Oh, what style! She launched herself like a sleek gazelle and seemed to hang suspended in the moist air like a finely sculptured statue of perfection... before belly flopping onto my head. I saw stars and not just the ones in the sky. But how could I not forgive her? She surfaced like a mermaid; her dark hair slick against her back and her dark t-shirt slick against her chest. We embraced, stripped and made steam.

Sunday 21 June

Dan was in a very good mood. He signed out a car and we drove to a garden centre in Be'er Sheva, a town not too far away. The kibbutz car we took was a Subaru – very popular in Israel. I had also seen some Escorts and Beetles. The Israelis go mad over the word 'Turbo' and stick it on everything with four wheels. During the drive I saw a Mini Turbo and an Escort Turbo which was in fact a 1.3 Popular. There were more boy-racers in Israel than in England.

I have to admit that I hated everything to do with gardening back home in Hertfordshire. But since doing the job on the kibbutz I was growing to like it and my seeds of enthusiasm were beginning to sprout. Dan and I strolled around the garden centre selecting plants and shrubs that were planned for certain areas of the kibbutz. He was starting to place a lot of trust in me, and it felt good to be given some responsibility. Dan said that I had to start at 5am the following morning because he wanted us to dig the holes for the new plants before it got too hot.

Beer and Bagels for Breakfast

Monday 22 June

4.45am: I'd just crawled out of bed. Einar was tossing and turning in his bed and mumbling some meaningless language. Probably Norwegian.

5am: Dan was sitting in the Noy shed drinking a cup of 'mud coffee', made by using filter coffee in the cup instead of ground coffee. It tasted very strong and, at the end, half of the cup contained a layer of 'mud' – hence the name. It was just getting light and the weather was still cool, so we took two shovels and loaded a wheelbarrows with the plants and went off to dig sixty holes, which took us about three hours.

8am: Breakfast break and I was starving. It was the best morning for the treat laid on by the kibbutz kitchen – fried eggs – it made a change from the usual salad. I filled my water bottle and joined Dan for the next stage of the job. We went around each of the holes we had dug, putting a plant in along with some fertiliser, which in fact cow dung from the dairy. Nothing was wasted on the kibbutz.

1pm: I finished work early, as I had to work again at night in the chickens.

10pm: Dana had told me this would be a crap job but I didn't really know what to expect. It was fowl. The chickens in two sheds had grown large enough to be transported to wherever they go to be killed. It was my job to get the chickens onto the lorries as quickly as possible. The only snag was that it had to be done in the dark so as not to panic the chickens. I found that quite ironic – they were going to the slaughterhouse, and the members didn't want them to feel uncomfortable. We were given a torch each, but we were only allowed to flick the light on for a couple of seconds at a time to see where the chickens were sitting. Then we had to grab four – yes, four – chickens in each hand by putting their legs through our fingers so they were hanging upside down. Once in my grasp, they would begin to wise up and would start to peck my hands, and to add to the fun and games, they were squirting shit down your arms.

The stench was beyond disgusting. I would have gagged but I had a mask over my nose and mouth to protect me from the feathers and sawdust that was floating in the air.

A small tractor-like vehicle was driving through the chickens with a shovel on the front, scooping the birds onto a conveyor belt. They travelled along the belt and ended up in cages at the back.

Some of the members were kicking the chickens into this machine and even swinging them around.

I saw some slower birds being crushed to death under the wheels or mutilated. I've never seen anything so sickening. I just wanted to get the job over with and go to have a shower.

The chickens were wide awake by now and squawking loudly. So much for the no-scare tactics.

It took about four hours to empty each shed. Then we had to go around and collect the bodies. There were quite a few splattered around the place.

Tuesday 23 June

I saw Dov at lunch and told him that I didn't want to do the chicken work again. He asked why and I said that it wasn't my idea of fun watching chickens getting squashed. He told me that every volunteer had to take a turn and I might be asked again. Not what I wanted to hear. Three more volunteers – three girls from Finland – arrived in the afternoon bringing the total on Naloz to twelve. I know that looks don't count for everything but I've seen more attractive walruses in London Zoo. And they were miserable. But coming from a freezing country where winter lasts for nine months is bound to affect one's state of mind, so I suppose they had some excuse. Their names were not suitably formed for the English tongue to pronounce; the closest I could get was Alien, Trog and Satsuma.

Wednesday 24 June

I received a letter from my mate Big Jack back in England. He's thirty-six years young and I'd known him since working for a local taxi company a few years back. Big Jack was a bit of a 'ducker and diver' but a totally good laugh. He wrote that he was having some money problems and that now would probably be a good time to 'get away for a bit', as the taxman, a loan company and his ex-wife were all ganging up on him.

He asked if I could arrange for him to come over to the kibbutz as a volunteer for about six months. It would be tricky, as the accepted age for volunteers is usually eighteen to thirty – I would have to grovel to Beatrice. She gave the okay, as long as Big Jack guaranteed to work hard. It seemed that volunteer age was less important than hard work.

4pm: Finished work late and wrote a letter back to Big Jack whilst lazing next to the pool. Told him the good news. The bad news was that there wasn't a bookie in sight.

Thursday 25 June

Alien, Trog and Satsuma started work in the dining room. I think that The Three Stooges could probably have made a better job of it. It must have been difficult for Heela (the member in charge of the dining room work) to explain what to do as the three Finnish girls didn't really speak much English.

Apparently Trog couldn't handle the automatic floor washer and had been dragged around behind it like someone taking a large disobedient dog for a walk. The floor was awash with soap suds at one stage, but with the help of Alien and Satsuma they'd managed to get it under control.

7pm: Went to Dana's and helped her cook a meal for the two of us. I was becoming an expert at Israeli cuisine and could now toss a mean salad with a deft flick of the wrist.

As the night was so warm we sat outside and shared some wine that I'd bought in the shop earlier: a cheeky little vintage with just a hint of strawberry and a nice fizz on the palate.

As we sipped, Dana whispered: 'You'll soon be hearing the patter of tiny feet around the place.'

After I'd finished choking on my wine I spluttered: 'Do you mean...?'

'Yes John,' Dana replied. 'I've decided to get some puppies. What do you think?'

'That I was about to have a heart attack,' I muttered under my breath.

Friday 26 June

Today, I had to go around the kibbutz and trim the date trees, using a vehicle that had three large tractor wheels and a platform that I could raise and lower according to the height of the tree, as I drove along. It was a bit like being on a very slow roller coaster. It took a bit of practice to manoeuvre it up to the side of a date tree, but was much quicker and easier than carrying a ladder around. Once I'd mastered it, there was no stopping me.

7pm: I sat with my KPs at the Shabbat meal and they told me that a group of Americans would soon be arriving to live on the kibbutz and do their army service.

They went on to explain that these Americans had been born in Israel but had moved to the States when very young. Although they weren't forced to do the army service, being Jewish they had chosen to do so.

It was quite a coup for Kibbutz Naloz to have them stay there as the Israeli government paid the kibbutz for the Americans' keep. A national newspaper also wanted to run a story about it and Naloz received quite a bit of publicity because of this. With over three hundred kibbutzim in Israel, standing out in any small distinctive way was beneficial.

11.30pm: Pub time. I stumbled upon a drinking contest taking place. The lucky contestants were Ben, Peter, Arthur, Einar, Alien, Trog and Satsuma.

The four blokes were slurring the merits of South Africa, Norway and Brazil in no particular order; the three Finnish females were downing vodka and cokes. They didn't seem pissed at all. Satsuma told me that because it was such a long winter in Finland there wasn't much to do and so a large amount of the population just drank. Hence the fact it took a large amount of alcohol to affect those three representatives. Suddenly there was a loud crash. Ben was flat on his back on the floor and laughing his head off. The contest winner!

Meanwhile the Israeli 'anthem' thumped from the loudspeakers: 'Sunday Bloody Sunday' by U2.

Saturday 27 June

Tonight would be the social event of the year – Arthur and myself were to be guest DJs in the Naloz pub! After lunch, we sacrificed our usual Saturday laze by the pool and went to the pub to get organised. There was certainly a good collection of music in the bar to choose from, which was enhanced with a selection of volunteers' personal tapes.

I'm quite good with electronics and electrical equipment and found the mixing deck very easy to operate. Arthur wasn't too sure

about it though and couldn't quite get the hang of smoothly intro-
ducing one track into another. There was a microphone attached to
the set-up that could be used for making announcements over the
music. This was going to be fun. Eventually Arthur got his act
together and we locked the pub up and gave the key back to the
bloke who ran it.

9pm: DJs Jazzy John and the Bad Brazilian strolled into the pub
like they owned the joint.

We checked that the 'wheels of steel' and the CD players were
cued up with the first few tracks. We didn't bother with a set list of
records but knew the sort of thing to keep the Israelis happy.

The Bad Brazilian's voice boomed from the loudspeakers: 'TEST-
ING...ONE...TWO...HELLOOOO...!' The bar staff were looking over
and laughing. I could see they were thinking, 'give the volunteers a
taste of power and they think they're God!'

Nearly right: we were Good.

10pm: DJ Jazzy John went to collect a couple of free beers from
the bar – one of the perks of being DJ on a Saturday night.
Meanwhile, the Bad Brazilian started to get the musical ball rolling.
He adjusted the odd dial, flicked a couple of switches and... the
lights went out. He'd accidentally hit the main power switch to the
pub. Our naff image took a further nosedive.

A few minutes later, DJ Jazzy John was at the helm and 'Shiny
Happy People' by REM flowed from the loudspeakers. The pub was
just starting to fill up with some members by now but the dance
floor was still empty. DJ Jazzy John and the Bad Brazilian were starting to get quite pissed; the free drinks were going down a treat: it
was thirsty work being hip.

11pm: The place began to buzz (just like my head). Lots of the
members and quite a few visitors were surging about on the dance
floor below us. My nerves had totally vanished.

I could just make out the volunteers sitting over in the darkened
corner at the far side of the pub. I gave them the thumbs up. Next
to me the Bad Brazilian was wildly shouting something over 'Peace
Frog' by The Doors – a real floor-filler in Naloz.

The raw, animal heat of the place and the large amounts of alcohol had combined to work their magic.

I switched on the microphone: 'WHO'S IN THE HOUSE...? ANY
JEWS IN THE HOUSE...? WHO – WHO – WHO'S IN THE HOUSE...?
ANY JEW – JEW – JEWS IN THE HOUSE...? HERE'S A SHOUT GOING

OUT TO THE KIBBUTZ NALOZ VOLUNTEERS FROM DJ JAZZY JOHN AND THE BAD BRAZILIAN...!!'

We were rocking now. 'Don't You Forget About Me' by Simple Minds faded out and The Cure's 'Killing An Arab' came on. Ben, Peter and Einar were bouncing around below us.

Microphone on: 'BEN YOU FAT BASTARD! PETE YOU UGLY GIT! ANY REQUESTS?'

Both shouted back in unison: 'Have you got 'Hang the DJ' by The Smiths?'

Sunday 28 June

Ho hum.

After my night of stardom it was back to being a mere volunteer and working for the collective good of the kibbutz. Galit, a mother-of-two, had joined as a permanent member of the Noy team along with Dan and myself. Her husband worked as a vet on the kibbutz and also in town. Members could have jobs outside the kibbutz but any income they made had to be donated to kibbutz funds. In this way, they still got all their food and housing bills paid, which seemed like a fair agreement.

Galit and I worked together to trim thick bushes that had grown past the windows of certain members' houses. The work was tough physically but it was also rewarding to see the results of our hard labour. Galit was really into sculptures and we managed to shape one very large bush to look like a giant cake with a cherry on the top. It wasn't all work and no play.

1pm: After lunch, Jenny and Linda left Kibbutz Naloz for England.

Their visas would have expired a few days later and they didn't want any hassle from the customs staff at Ben-Gurion Airport. They went through the dining room saying tearful farewells to their favourite members (and past boyfriends).

We swapped addresses and promised to get in touch for a reunion when I returned to the homeland. I asked them to send me a bacon sandwich. We chatted a little about the good times, the bad times, the laughter and the tears. They took off and that left yours truly as the only English volunteer on Naloz.

Beer and Bagels for Breakfast

Tuesday 30 June

I felt like death warmed up. Two days of sickness.
Roy Orbison happened to be crooning on the radio and my belly was gurgling along to 'I'm Hurtin".

JULY

Wednesday 1 July

Feeling better, I returned to work. Dan was fine about my absence. The members did not seem to mind volunteers having days off sick, as long as they didn't take advantage and drag it out.

I began in the morning with one of my favourite jobs: cutting the grass. On with the shades and I was revving up and raring to get started.

1pm: All the volunteers were gathered together at lunch and introduced to our new volunteer leader called Rena. She was about twenty and very friendly. Apparently Beatrice had enough of the job and the hassles that went with it.

Thursday 2 July

5am: I was 'on loan' to work in the fields – hence the early start to beat the heat. My job was to drive a tractor out to one of the fields and along with two members collect the very large irrigation pipes.

It was very tiring work – while one person drove the tractor slowly along the furrows of the field, the other two had to run, slip and slide in the mud, unscrew the pipes and hoist them onto the trailer at the rear of the tractor. The pipes were full of water and were very slippery with mud, which made them very heavy to lift and drain. After a couple of hours on the job, I realised how lucky I was to be a 'Noynik' (Noy employee).

8pm: The volunteers had a barbecue on the lawn outside the rooms. Hot beers and cold girls (or was it vice versa?). Satsuma and Alien did the cooking whilst Mette took charge of the potatoes, while Ben, Peter and Einar finished off a bottle of cheap Israeli brandy.

It was the closest thing to 'Jack Daniels' I could find that was sold on the kibbutz. We invited Rena over and a few of the younger Israelis, who all brought food and drink with them. Dana also came over and brought her camera to take some snaps for posterity. It was an excellent night. But the best thing was that living in the same place as we partied meant that we didn't have to go home at the end of the night.

Beer and Bagels for Breakfast

Friday 3 July

Shabbat already! The days were flying past – I'd been on the kibbutz for about two months. Whilst it didn't seem that long, there was never a moment when I could forget I was in the Middle East because of the news.

There was a story in The Jerusalem Post that day about a young Israeli soldier who was kidnapped and killed by members of an Arab terrorist organisation. He was only nineteen years old and had been hitchhiking to his home kibbutz from the army base where he was stationed.

Saturday 4 July

11am: Woke up with Dana and a hangover. I couldn't remember anything that happened in the pub the previous night – it must have been a good one.

11.04am: Went into the bathroom for a pee and discovered that I was minus one eyebrow...

'Ben and Pete are DEAD MEN!!!'

1pm: Confronted the terrible twins at lunch and they confessed to doing the dirty deed. I started planning my revenge campaign. I went to my KPs' house for the rest of the afternoon and watched a video and some MTV whilst scoffing cream cakes and lashings of ginger pop. Bliss. They asked where my eyebrow was and I spun them a tale about English custom and sacrifice in the name of male virility. I don't think they believed me.

8pm: Dana was working the late shift at the laundry. She would be finished an hour later so we could go to Stirot and one of the clubs. She gave me an extra electric fan so that Einar and myself could have one each. Little luxuries like that meant a lot in the life of a kibbutz volunteer.

9.30pm: Off to Stirot. We booked a minibus to take us to town and chipped in for petrol expenses.

There was Dana, Ben, Peter, Arthur, Mette, Dorte and Trog and myself. The other volunteers decided to stay back for the kibbutz pub.

We hung out in The Warehouse all night because there was a great atmosphere. Beers were only four shekels a bottle, which was cheaper than normal for some reason. I could see a lot of volunteers from Gerim and other kibbutzim in the area so we joined up with them and let our hair down.

Luckily it was quite dark and the lasers were flashing about in the club so my tiny (embarrassing) lack of facial hair went unnoticed by anyone else.

Sunday 5 July

6am: I had to do Ben's job in the kitchen because he was laid up in bed with a bad case of 'hangover-itis'. His job comprised of taking delivery of the food, cleaning out the large fridges and meat freezer and generally being a gofer, seeking out anything that the women cooking the food needed.

Sometimes a few of the women might start arguing over how a recipe should be prepared or something trivial. I thought that I'd heard some rackets in my time but nothing comes close to two Israeli women having a slanging match!

As the kibbutz cook, Guy was the big cheese as far as controlling the kitchen staff went – and he ruled with a rod of spaghetti. He wasn't afraid to shout at the women who worked in the kitchen in order to get the culinary results that he wanted. But after each spat, everyone was the best of friends once more in a matter of minutes. That seemed to be the prevailing philosophy: speak your mind and get everything out into the open.

I was 'well in' with the lady who ran the dairy shop and every time I took her delivery she gave me the pick of the yoghurt shelf. I was like a greedy kid in a sweet shop. There was strawberry, banana and apricot. Oh joy...even chocolate!

Then I witnessed one of the rare low points of my kibbutz experience.

Guy took delivery of some live fish and I had to help him unload them from the lorry that had brought them straight from market. He said that they had to be de-scaled before gutting and cooking. He switched on the potato-peeling machine, which looked rather like an upturned tumble dryer. The difference was that it had an abrasive drum that water was pumped into through a hose. As the potatoes swirled around, the skins would be scrubbed off and washed out with the dirty water.

One guess where the fish were going...

The machine shook and vibrated as the fish spun around in a

silvery whirlpool. It was disgusting. Scales were pouring out from the waste pipe, along with eyes and fins. I thought that the chicken shed spectacle was gross but this really made me want to gag. A few minutes later, the peeler was switched off and the fish cascaded out. They were barely alive and minus their scales. Their heads were then cut off, and they were finally gutted.

I mused that next time Ben had a day off Einar should replace him – he probably would have bought tickets for a spectacle like that.

Tuesday 7 July

Got a letter from Big Jack. He was selling his car and had booked a flight to Israel on 23 July.

Wednesday 8 July

The twenty American teenagers arrived for their three-year stay on the kibbutz to do their army service. After they completed their army service, they had the option to become permanent and full time members of the kibbutz, if they wanted to. After coming from the 'bright lights – big city' of American life, it would probably take them some time to get used to the quieter pace of life at Naloz, and so they would be working like the volunteers for the first few weeks before enlisting in the army.

Because this was to be their home for the next few years they would be living in slightly better accommodation than we would. Their rooms included fridges, bathrooms, small kitchens and televisions. Actually, coming to think of it, they had much better accommodation than us volunteers!

Thursday 9 July

7am: I was left in charge of the Noy today, as Dan and Galit went to the garden centre. My first job was to trim the branches of some small trees and paint the stumps with a special chemical to prevent them growing back again. There were some good songs playing on the radio that morning. The Voice of Peace, a pirate radio ship is anchored off the coast of Tel Aviv, and it broadcasts mainly in English. If there happened to be a radio nearby, you could bet that the volunteers would be listening to it. In any one hour, you could hear anything from John Lennon to Pearl Jam, The Carpenters to Crowded House. The DJs were a little amateurish, but they did their best. And I mean that sincerely, folks.

9pm: A pool party for the volunteers, Americans and most of the kibbutz's young Israelis.

The Americans supplied the music; mainly rock with a smattering of metal. Just the right mixture to crank the volume up. At least here there was no such thing as an irate banging on the wall and shouting: 'Oi you young hooligan! Turn that bloody racket down before I 'ave yer!'

After the food and drinks were consumed everyone fell (or were thrown) into the pool fully clothed. A game of no-rules water polo soon developed and was vigorously contested.

The result of these high jinks was that an American bloke called Mike bravely – nay – feebly tried to hold onto the ball for too long. He ended up with a burst eardrum and had to be taken to hospital by ambulance.

11.30pm: Everyone went home except the trusty volunteers who indulged in some skinny-dipping.

Friday 10 July

Mike was released from hospital after being kept in overnight. He was okay, but just a little bit hard of hearing. I said: HE WAS OKAY, BUT JUST A LITTLE BIT HARD OF HEARING!

The kibbutz garage had repaired a moped for the Noy staff. It was called a 'tus-tus' for some bizarre reason, had a basket on the back for tools and a top speed of about thirty miles per hour. I already had my own bicycle that I'd previously acquired from Dan's workshop but the tus-tus was faster and more fun. Now I volunteered to go back and forth from the Noy shed to collect things: 'Oh damn. I've accidentally on purpose forgotten to bring that packet of seeds. I had better take the tus-tus to fetch them...!'

7.30pm: At the Shabbat meal the Americans sang a Hebrew song. I sat with my KPs and their two-year-old son (my kibbutz brother). He conducted the music by merrily splashing his spoon into the chicken soup and sending noodles every which way.

The main course was schnitzels (a Jewish regular), potatoes (an Irish regular), vegetables (a caterpillar's regular) and a glass of red wine (a French regular). I smothered mine in tomato sauce as usual (a combination to make me go regular). At the end of the meal I spied Satsuma discreetly smuggling a bottle of white wine out with all the panache of a shoplifter.

9.30pm: Ben had concocted a great punch from orange juice, vodka and white rum. The volunteers whiled away the hours before the pub opened with the punch, whilst playing the game where you have to try and guess the name of a famous person stuck on your forehead.

In two surreal hours I became Frankenstein, Margaret Thatcher and Vlad the Impaler. The similarities between each one made them easy to guess.

11.30pm: Routine pub. Shouted, drank, danced and collapsed.

Saturday 11 July

Woke up and felt on top of the world. That was a nice change for a Saturday morning – it was usually a thumping head and somersaulting stomach. The birds were singing and the sun was bright, so I put my swimming shorts on and jogged to the pool like a fitness freak.

There wasn't anyone about so I clambered over the fence and indulged in a few press-ups using just my thumbs. Then feeling nicely loose I hooked my ankles around a bench and knocked off a couple of hundred vertical sit-ups. Whistling to myself, I ran a couple of laps around the swimming pool and then dived in. It felt like heaven. The cool water enveloped my sweating body like a fly that has fallen into a tub of ice cream.

I powered through eighty lengths like a salmon swimming for its spawning ground. This was a new me. I felt healthy, fit and relaxed. At one with nature and the beautiful world that...

11.30am: Einar shook me awake and told me it was nearly time for lunch. My head thumped and my stomach was turning somersaults.

2 pm: The Yanks thrashed us at softball without breaking sweat. To them it was just a slower version of baseball – which they were good at anyway. They seemed to whack every ball for miles and it just guided itself to their waiting gloves when they fielded.

9pm: Dana was pissed off with me for getting wrecked last night. I told her that Englishmen enjoyed the occasional tipple and one day I would outgrow it. She didn't believe me, so we stayed in and popped olives from each other's belly buttons.

Sunday 12 July

It was back to the waste pit in the fields this morning to dump a load of dead bushes and a large container load of rubbish and rotting food from the kitchens. At the pit, I put the tractor into reverse and slowly inched back down the treacherous slope. When I reached the bottom, I noticed the dead cow still there in the water, and tried not to look too closely. I undid the chain on the food container, which toppled onto its side and spewed forth a cascade of meat, vegetable peel, eggs, fish and tin cans and other savoury items of delight. I then had to use a shovel to scrape the rest of the crap out. The stench was unimaginable.

Once I'd finished, I hooked the container back onto the tractor, eased into first gear and started to edge up the slope. The wheels were now wet, and had started to spin in the mud, losing their grip. Halfway up the slope, the tractor decided to gracefully slip back down again. All attempts to gain traction with some old packing crates under the wheels failed miserably – all I managed to do was push the crates deep into the churned mud.

Fucking great! I was stuck in a stinking food pit, the sun beat down mercilessly and flies were trying to make nests in my ears and nostrils. Just then I heard the sound of an engine coming over the hill. Saved!

I gingerly picked my way up the slope and saw a large blue tractor coming towards the pit. There were four Arab workers riding on it. Would they help me or drive straight past? Luckily they stopped for me.

They couldn't speak English but could see the trouble I was having. They tied a strong rope to the back of their tractor and to the front of mine. They revved up the engine and towed me out of the pit of doom in a flash. I could sense they thought it was funny by the way they were laughing at my predicament and shitty clothes and boots. I sheepishly thanked them and drove back to the kibbutz.

What a way to start the week.

Beer and Bagels for Breakfast

Monday 13 July

At breakfast, Mette and Dorte came to tell me they were going to Stirot that afternoon. It was about time for a haircut so I said I'd go with them for the ride.

I met up with Dan and Galit, after breakfast, to help them repair some irrigation pipes near the kibbutz main office that was the control centre where the money was handled and phone calls received. The Secretary of the Kibbutz worked from this office and (s)he was elected by the other members every few years – depending on how good a job they happened to be doing.

The office contained a safe where we could store valuable items like passports and traveller's cheques, but there were only certain days when volunteers could change money or retrieve their passports. On Kibbutz Naloz it was Tuesday and Saturday mornings. And who were we to argue, missus?

3pm: Boarded the bus with Mette and Dorte to Stirot. I liked the way that Israeli buses played music during journeys. It drowned out the cranking of the gears. The two Swedish girls headed for the shops and I went to get my hair cut.

Tuesday 14 July

I had to dig an obscene amount of holes at work today. We had to lay a main water pipe alongside a path to supply lawn sprinklers for a new area recently cleared of very large cactii. To excavate the trench, which was about 50 metres long and a metre deep, we used a small mechanical digger which we had to fix into place every few metres, and then we had to shovel out the excess soil manually with a shovel. I was pouring with sweat, and the heat was intense.

4pm: Even though we finished late, the trench was still not finished – it would probably take a few days yet. Volunteers certainly earned their keep.

8pm: Went to Dana's for a mini-barbecue. After a little smooching, we played with her puppies, Rotem and Lalouche. Kibbutz life was heaven for old people, children and pets because they didn't have any worries at all and were looked after properly. Dana cooked a mean hamburger, which I polished off in no time. It was becoming harder to remind myself that I was still only a visitor to Israel.

Wednesday 15 July

6am: Continued digging the trench for the new water pipe. Although I wasn't afraid of hard work, I was easily bored by monotonous jobs like this one.

1pm: At lunch, Ben told me that Einar had left the kibbutz and gone travelling. The only person he'd said goodbye to was Beatrice.

I ran back to my room and checked that all my stuff was still there. It wasn't an ideal situation when the person sharing your room suddenly does a bunk without telling a soul. All my belongings were intact, including my beer supply and collection of tapes. Phew.

It was good news in a way because Big Jack would be able to share with me when he arrived from London. I went back to the dining room for a quick cup of tea before resuming the dreaded digging.

Now there were nine volunteers: Ben, Peter, Mette, Dorte, Arthur, Alien, Trog and Satsuma and myself.

Thursday 16 July

2pm: Finished the fucking trench at last. What a job that was!

Later on, us volunteers felt like doing something stupid for a change - we put on odd shoes (like a flip-flop and a work boot) and traipsed over to the dining room for the evening meal. The members asked us what we were doing.

We told them we were celebrating All Shoes Eve, a traditional English holiday whereby odd footwear had to be worn. This would guarantee good luck for the coming year and make our journey through life that much smoother and richer. We must have looked a right load of plonkers.

Friday 17 July

7am: What a lovely end to the working week: cutting the grass around the swimming pool. The lifeguard never unlocked the gates until 10am so I had the whole place to myself. I've always wanted my own swimming pool and for a few hours I had it. Hot and sweaty, I walked too close to the edge of the water and – whoops, silly me – fell in.

Beer and Bagels for Breakfast

10am: Mid-morning tea break with Dan and Galit in the Noy hut. We always had some sort of cake on Fridays because of Shabbat. It wasn't unusual for other members to join us if they were passing by for a drink and gossip. I didn't know what the hell they were jabbering about though because it was mostly in Hebrew. I was beginning to pick up the odd phrase here and there and could sometimes work out the gist of what the Israelis were talking about. (It was handy to learn the Hebrew word for 'volunteer'.)

1pm: Fun and games over, it was time for some grub. The food was always light at this time of day on Shabbat because of the larger meal to come later on in the evening. I had some sort of watery stew with a generous dollop of mash on top. The other volunteers were sitting on the usual table in the middle and gossiping about why Einar had suddenly left.

Being his roommate they asked me, but I didn't have the faintest idea. Who knows what goes on in a Norwegian's mind when there's a full moon in Israel? Spooky.

9pm: Us volunteers waved our arms in the air and partied like we just didn't care. All of us, that is except Mette and Dorte who took offence at the drunken shouting emanating from Satsuma's room where everyone had gathered.

Ben and Peter took offence at Mette and Dorte's offence and staggered to the Swedish girls' room armed with a tube of glue. This was turning ugly. There's nothing worse than a pissed South African with a tube of glue and a bad attitude. Peter stuck the nozzle in the lock and filled it with glue. I hoped the girls still didn't have the key in the other side or they'd be trapped

11pm: The Swedish girls didn't show up for the pub. I could see how pissed Ben and Peter were by now so it would be a good night to get some sweet revenge for my absent eyebrow. I enlisted the assistance of Arthur and waited until the South Africans rolled back to their room. We waited twenty minutes, and then crept in to hear them both snoring loudly. Armed with shaving foam and razors, Arthur and myself separated Ben and Peter from their eyebrows. Ben also lost his moustache and had it stuck to the wall with the rest of the glue. Then a few quick photos were taken with shaving foam on heads for posterity.

Saturday 18 July

1pm: It was really funny at lunch when Ben and Pete wandered
into the dining room and sat at the volunteers' table. They accused
me of doing the dirty deed. I held up my hands and pleaded tempo-
rary insanity. Luckily they saw the joke.

Uncle Dov, the work manager came to the table and informed
all the volunteers that we'd be working in the watermelon fields
with the Americans the following Monday.

After lunch, we took the Noy tractor out for a jaunt to the fields
with beer, food, a cassette player and some Israelis. The heat was
intense and the sun made the alcohol go to our heads. The bare
skin above Pete and Ben's eyes started to go red and burn in the
sun.

Sunday 19 July

Dan wasn't too happy about me being away from the Noy for
two days but the watermelons took priority now. The work manager had no choice but to juggle people around to cover all the jobs
that needed doing every week.

Monday 20 July

4.55am: Yawning constantly, I made my way over to the tractor
sheds where the watermelon workers had to meet. Before I'd even
got there I could hear the yacking of the Yanks breaking the peace
of the still air.

The other bleary-eyed volunteers turned up and we all had a
quick cup of strong mud coffee. In all, there were about fifty workers milling around consisting of members, Americans, Arabs, a
couple of dogs and us volunteers (on the bottom rung of the
kibbutz social 'ladder').

We all climbed into an assortment of trucks and cars and sped
out to the watermelon fields. Sitting on the back of a truck at that
time of the morning was very chilly.

The dogs ran around and chased small watermelons thrown by
some of the members. The mood was excellent because people
were working alongside others that they might never have worked
with before, or even knew. I got to know a few people that I'd seen

every day on the kibbutz but never actually had a conversation with.

8am: Time for breakfast. Our team had already filled three trucks, which was apparently about average.

4pm: Still not finished – we had to work a couple of hours more lining up the best watermelons in the field for collection the following morning. It was murder working in this heat, when the swimming pool was calling me, but that was part of the working routine that goes with the watermelon job. It's only five hours' work but split into two halves.

11.29pm: Made love with Dana...

11.30 pm: Sleep.

Wednesday 22 July

Made arrangements with Dov to have Thursday off so that I could surprise Big Jack and meet him at Ben-Gurion Airport. He wasn't very good with directions; after all, he had been a taxi driver.

Thursday 23 July

Big Jack's flight was scheduled to arrive in Tel Aviv at 2pm. I loved Tel Aviv and it was great to be heading back there again on a beautiful sunny day. The air conditioning was blasting through the bus, the radio was loud and I was due to meet a good mate of mine. The world was alright with me!

11.30am: As usual, the Central Bus Station was a hive of activity with shoppers, tourists and soldiers scurrying in every direction. That was the only place I've ever been to where it was possible to buy anything from bagels to prostitutes to tacky posters of Sly Stallone all in the same location. Reached Ben-Gurion forty minutes later. There was still about an hour to go before Big Jack landed so I went and bought a McDavids, which is was the Israeli equivalent of McDonalds but not as good. In fact, it tasted McShit. Being at the airport reminded me that my visa would expire on Tuesday August 4. I had to remember to renew it. The arrivals board confirmed that Big Jack's flight had landed in the Holy Land so I went to meet him at the gate. Big Jack had arrived for the party!

And God said: 'Let there be two likely London lads loose in the land of milk and lager,' and lo and behold, this came to pass.

Friday 24 July

Big Jack was sharing my room so I tried to be quiet when setting out for work. He'd met all the other volunteers the previous evening and had expressed surprise at the paltry meal that we got served at that time of night.

2pm: Finished work and gave Big Jack a whistle-stop tour of Naloz because Rena was busy. Filled him in with the details of free beer, wages allowance and where the swimming pool was. All the important stuff.

3pm: Lazed by the pool for a couple of hours and wondered if I'd looked as white as Big Jack when I had first arrived on the kibbutz. He made Barbara Cartland look tanned.

8pm: Sat with my KPs at the Shabbat meal. They would be Big Jack's 'parents' also – which was weird as he's older than both of them!

10pm: Drinking games in the Swedish girls' room, which doubled as an initiation ceremony for Big Jack. Obscene amounts of alcohol and loud music flowed freely and we played our part in reducing the EU's wine lake somewhat.

11.30pm: It was great to have another British volunteer on site at pub time. Imagine, if you will, two lager louts in a strange land who have entered the...Cliche Zone. 'Ere we go, ere we go, ere we go... down it in one ya wanker... shit I'm pissed...'

Saturday 25 July

Most of the volunteers, including myself, had a one-way ticket to Hangover City. I went to Dana's, took two headache tablets and fell asleep on her bed.

7pm: Dana woke me up in time for dinner. I was in a really grumpy mood because I hated wasting our only day off doing sweet Fanny Adams. At least my head was clear. Big Jack met Dov and was told that he would be working in the kitchens, receiving the deliveries and getting the girls what they required.

11pm: I stuck to Dana like chewing gum to hair because I felt that we hadn't been seeing eye-to-eye recently. The pub was full to the brim with Yanks, volunteers, Israelis and one of the kibbutz dogs had made a guest appearance before being chased out. Big Jack was finding his feet and chatting to a girl that always visited from a neighbouring kibbutz. Should I have told him that she was a lesbian?

Sunday 26 July

Every Sunday morning, without fail, the same thought came to mind as I dragged myself from bed: if I was in England now I could stay in bed for the rest of the day. But this was Israel. There was grass to be cut, weeds to be pulled and a dozen other gardening jobs to do. Catching a glimpse of the glorious sunshine outside spurred me on slightly.

1pm: Met up with Big Jack at lunch. He said that the kitchen job was pretty strenuous to begin with but he was sure to get into the swing of things soon. He'd got to know a few more members during the morning's work, and found most of them to be friendly after resorting to his 'C.C.C.' (Cockney Chappie Chat).

Monday 27 July

A baby boy was circumcised in the Members' Club today, and the volunteers were invited. The place was filled with the baby's family and guests, and there was a celebratory air to proceedings. This was obviously very different to the sort of 'day out' that I was used to in England. Even so, it was all over in the flash of an eye. The man performing the snip placed a pincer-like clamp in the appropriate place, snapped his fingers and before you could say 'no jacket required' – it was done. Drinks were served and party nibbles passed around. I politely declined the nuts.

Wednesday 29 July

Volunteer flags were lowered to half-mast to mark the departure of those cultural cool dudes, Ben and Peter. They planned to head for Greece and attempt to find work in a bar for the remainder of the summer. When they left, the remaining eight volunteers formed an 'arch of honour' with empty beer bottles outside their room, and Ben and Pete walked through it like a tunnel. Addresses were swapped in the unspoken knowledge that we'd never see each other again. It was just one of those kibbutz consequences. You meet some great people and then they're gone.

AUGUST

Saturday 1 August

I ran my hangover off during a game of football with the kibbutz members. Most of the teams in the Israeli football league are sponsored by companies, and so many are named after companies or products, as in the case of Maccabi Tel Aviv, (sponsored by a beer company). Many young kibbutz members followed English clubs, in particular Manchester United (sad fools). English league results were published every Sunday in The Jerusalem Post.

After our little kibbutz match, Guy donated some steaks to the volunteers, which we decided to barbecue before the pub opened. We invited the Americans and young members of the kibbutz. The 'entrance fee' was a couple of bottles of beer. It was the sort of gathering I enjoyed most in the course of the year – despite our different backgrounds, no one was an outsider, and everyone mixed well.

Sunday 2 August

5am: Working in the fields – absolute murder after a late Saturday night. I was still drunk, but drove a tractor in a convoy of four others along a very narrow dirt track out to the fields, although thankfully I wasn't heading the line.

In England I had never driven under the influence, but somehow a tractor on a sunny kibbutz seemed different – perhaps less dangerous? It took us twenty minutes to reach the cornfields, where we had to push our way through to the middle of the crop to retrieve irrigation pipes and machinery that was needed elsewhere. It didn't sound too strenuous, but it was! The pipes were several feet long, and the machinery felt like it weighed a ton, that is, once we'd found it in the 'jungle' of corn. Carrying it all out was not easy as the plants blocked the way and snagged our arms and ankles – tripping up and getting whacked in the eye with cobs of corn seemed to be the order of the day. The consolation was that we could eat all the fresh, juicy corn we wanted.

Monday 3 August

Big Jack confided in me that he'd scored with Mette on Saturday after the pub closed. He had certainly kept that one close to his chest. Sly git!

Beer and Bagels for Breakfast

Tuesday 4 August

Day off – so I made for Ashlekon, where I could renew my visa. The town did not look too impressive, although apparently there was a great beach there, which I planned to check out after completing my business. Following Rena's directions, it took me about forty minutes to locate the Israeli equivalent of the Ministry of Interior. Climbing the two flights of stairs and past a security guard with the customary holstered weapon, it struck me that it was amazing how quickly a tourist can become used to seeing firearms in everyday use.

There were about six office clerks on the right of the room sitting behind desks and three times as many citizens waiting to see them. I found the room for volunteer visas and met the woman with whom I would be having some great verbal battles with over the coming months. Her gaze could freeze Death Valley.

To cut a long story short, she renewed my visa for another three months and also renewed my view that some Israelis in officialdom can be very rude and arrogant. I left and caught a bus to the famed beach, which lived up to its reputation. I put a knotted handkerchief on my head, rolled up my jeans and went for a paddle in the cool sea. Aye, it were grand!

Thursday 6 August

I couldn't believe that I'd been here for a quarter of a year already.

Friday 7 August

It was the end of the Swedish volunteers' stay on Naloz. Yes, Mette and Dorte left for pastures new. It meant that I was now the longest-serving volunteer on Kibbutz Naloz, for what it was worth. It also meant that there were only six of us now: Big Jack Arthur Trog Alien Satsuma and me. The Swedish girls forgot that they had ten shekels left on their shop card so the rest of us bought a bottle of brandy and toasted them in their absence before the pub opened.

Saturday 8 August

After lunch Arthur and myself joined in a game of 'no rules water polo'. Big Jack can't swim so had to watch from the sidelines. Arthur got swamped by three Israeli soldiers and did a brilliant impression of a drowning Brazilian. August is the hottest time of year in Israel and the sun was absolutely scorching. I've never felt heat like it in my life and wished we had two days off a week to enjoy.

Arthur and I were totally brown, Big Jack was on his way – but the Finnish Three were still very pasty.

11pm: The volunteers from Kibbutz Gerim turned up for the pub with a few of their Israeli mates. We had a good laugh and they invited us to go with them to a nightclub the following Saturday.

Sunday 9 August

A new helper joined us in the Noy. His name was Ish – a student from a local college and a right prat into the bargain, but thankfully he would only be helping out on Sundays.

The two of us had to trim some palm trees, whose fronds had been intruding onto the roofs and windows of some members' houses. Ish was ordering me around as if he was the boss, and that he knew everything about gardening. It was a bit like me trying to advise Oliver Reed on how to sup a pint.

I put up with it for a couple of hours just to keep the peace, but then I'd had enough – Dan was the only one who could tell me what to do. I politely told him that he wasn't my boss and that I knew enough about the job to carry it out properly. He went on the defensive and droned on about how much he wanted to be the manager of his own gardening centre in the future.

Yes, yes, very nice... now get on with the practical part of your studying.

When work was finished for the day Dan and Galit told me that they didn't think much of him either – but another pair of hands was always welcome considering that we only had a regular Noy team of three people.

Beer and Bagels for Breakfast

Monday 10 August

Ploughing is one of my favourite jobs, and it was made all the more enjoyable for borrowing a tractor from the team that worked in the almonds. It was a small blue Italian job with an enclosed cab, air conditioning and controls and it could turn on a shekel. It was the Rolls Royce of the tractor world. The only things it needed to complete the image were a thousand-watt stereo, furry dice and maybe 'Turbo' plastered on the back (you can't buy class). Dan gave me the afternoon off as I had accomplished so much in the morning, so Dana and I played a game of tennis. Did I mention – any potential volunteers reading this – that most kibbutzim have their own free tennis courts?

Tuesday 11 August

5am: So that was why Dan was so lenient the previous day – an early start today. (Crafty sod.)

It was time to spray the weeds again and banish them to burn in Shrub Hell.

Wednesday 12 August

I was in a philosophical mood and delving into the fluff of my mind's belly button thinking about the volunteers that had come and gone...

Life is like a train journey. Hopefully it will be a long and eventful one, but after a while, you can't recall where you boarded. Certain people will begin that journey with you, but not last the distance. Others will accompany you for the whole trip, and you may even travel further than them.

Yet more passengers will get on at various stages and others may realise that they have reached their stop, and depart. Quite often the train will run into the sidings or hit trouble – then you should put your faith in the driver to see you through.

But don't ever jump off a moving train, no matter how long the tunnel seems to last. There is always light at the end of it. The scenery that you pass through should remain in your memory forever, even when it's something that you would rather not witness. If you have bought the right ticket, then the journey should pass happily and with success. Above all, you should bear in mind the destination that you hope to eventually reach.

Wow. Where did all that come from?

Thursday 13 August

Rena told us that there would be a trip to Jerusalem in September.

Friday 14 August

The week seemed to fly by so quickly. I couldn't wait for the night out to a nearby town called Rehovot that we were planning on Saturday.

I chugged around the kibbutz on the tractor sunning myself, working under my own initiative and at my own pace. Big Jack had a day off and I could see him dipping his feet into the pool as I drove by. He should try and learn to swim while he was on the kibbutz.

I made a detour to the laundry to collect my clean clothes and see Dana. She wanted to come with me on Saturday night. I asked if she had any girlfriends that she could ask along who might get on with Big Jack and Arthur and she promised to try and sort something out.

11pm: Had a drinking contest with the other volunteers in the pub. I must admit the Finnish Three held their own, but Arthur just managed to nick it at the last moment with a late burst of rum and coke.

In victory, he tried to gargle the Brazilian national anthem but ended up gargling with his dinner.

Saturday 15 August

Big Jack sloped into the room early in the morning. I put him on the spot and he said that a girl in the pub had invited him to her room. Jammy dodger!

9pm: The Kibbutz Gerim volunteers picked six of us up in a minibus and we were off to a town called Rehovot. There was me, Dana, Big Jack, the girl he'd become acquainted with, Arthur and a girlfriend of Dana's called Titse. (Weird name; nice girl.) The Gerim bunch said that they'd been to the club before and that it was excellent, and they were right – it was a great place. Expensive (twenty-five shekels to get in/six shekels a beer), loud, a good light show and a dance floor like a sardine tin.

Sunday 16 August

A weird thing happened today. I was sitting with Bog Hack outside our room, when a white horse trotted right past us. It wasn't the sort of thing one would expect to see in Israel at about nine o'clock of an evening. Five minutes later it walked past us in the opposite direction as calm as you please. My first thought was that someone had slipped a tab of acid in my beer and that I was hallucinating, but when a naked Demi Moore and a jar of whipped cream failed to materialise I had to reconsider. My more prosaic explanation was that it had somehow escaped from the children's zoo and was going walkabout. This proved to be true when the girl who looked after the zoo went tearing past about ten minutes later asking us if we'd happened to see a horse.

Big Jack and I nodded like a couple of Thunderbirds puppets.

Monday 17 August

Rena sprung a fantastic surprise on us – because there were so few volunteers on Naloz the members decided to move us to better rooms. The only catch was that if anybody from outside the kibbutz wanted to rent the rooms then we had to move back pronto, as the kibbutz obviously couldn't afford to lose money. I would share with Big Jack, the Finnish Three were in a room together and Arthur was by himself. The rooms were luxurious – can you believe we each had our own fridge?! It got even better: we even had our own toilet and shower rooms. And a sink. And a kettle. I couldn't take this extravagance after the 'jail cells'. Were we worthy? I felt like the fictional kid who'd gained a golden ticket and was off to Willy Wonka's chocolate factory.

The rooms were in a terrace over the far side of the kibbutz, so it meant a slightly longer walk to the dining room, not that I was complaining. However, the cow sheds were nearby but today the wind was blowing in a favourable direction. After work, I borrowed the tractor from the Noy and attached the trailer to carry all the volunteers' belongings over in one trip.

August

11pm: Big Jack, Arthur, Trog, Alien, Satsuma and yours truly sat outside and toasted our new terrace. We christened it The Valley (a combination of 'volunteer alley').

Tuesday 18 August

Forgive me Father for I have sinned. Well... sort of.
There was a big delivery of food and drink to the kibbutz kitchens today and Big Jack was asked to carry it all to the storage area. Dodgy choice of volunteer. Included in the consignment was a regular order of thirty crates of Carlsberg beer destined for the pub. Big Jack secreted a crate in the bushes near to the storeroom when the coast was clear.
11.30pm: We transported the crate to our new room. At the last count there were six beers in our fridge.
Now it totalled fifty-four bottles of ice-cold bliss.

Wednesday 19 August

Bit of a boring day. More or less the mundane nine-to-five routine. You know: eating... swimming... sunbathing... drinking...
9pm: Big Jack and I left the door open to let the mosquitoes in just so that we could hunt and squash them for something to do. I managed to track and squash a large bounder that had settled for a breather on a poster of Jim Morrison (being used to cover up a crack in the wall). It looked as though the Lizard King had popped a large zit on his nose.

Thursday 20 August

Each volunteer had to work an occasional turn in the chicken sheds, and today it was my privilege once more. I finished in the Noy at about 3pm and rode the scooter to the sheds, expecting the worst after my last experience. This time is was quite different, as the kibbutz was taking a delivery of young chicks that they would fatten up. The lorries transporting them backed up to the large doors of the shed and all the lights were switched off, to ensure that the chicks were kept as calm as possible. Inside were rows of circular pens with water bottles and gas lamps to keep the chicks warm. These pens ran the length of the shed, and the combined heat of all the lamps was sweltering. I had to carry four cardboard trays of chicks into the shed at a time, and I had to put twenty trays into each pen. As I carried them, the chicks stared me in the eye from their trays, bobbing their heads up and down in time with my footsteps, cheeping incessantly. The worst part of the day's work had to be the heat, as well as the smell that clung to my clothes and hair.

Friday 21 August

Shabbat Shalom! (Hello Shabbat!)
A new volunteer arrived on the scene. He came from France and his name was Frank – honestly – it was 'French Frank'. He shared Arthur's room in The Valley. Frank would be working in the dining room ('ze 'orrible crap job') as the members were always eagerly looking for new recruits there.

9pm: After dinner there was some traditional Israeli dancing outside the dining room. Dana persuaded me to have a go and I was awful.

The participants dance around in a large circle formation, while spinning about at the same time. I don't know how they remembered all the steps, because they came fast and furious. I got totally confused and ended up doing a poor imitation of the Birdie Dance. But, when in Rome...!

Saturday 22 August

Guy the cook came over to our table at lunch to have a word with Big Jack. The words 'crate of beer' and 'missing' instantly sprang to mind. Since Guy represented a Mafia Don as far as the kibbutz hierarchy was concerned, this wasn't too comforting.

'Can you please start work at 5 o'clock tomorrow, Jack?' Phew.

Sunday 23 August

Ish the wanker helped us in the Noy again. I can honestly say that since arriving in Israel all those months ago he was the only real bell-end that I'd had the misfortune to meet. He was trying to show me how to do some work that I had been getting on with perfectly well for weeks.

'No, do it this way... that's wrong... this is right...' Ish didn't let up.

I planned the following week to take him out and introduce him to the dead cow in the dump. Head first.

Monday 24 August

Frank wasn't too impressed. The dishwasher broke down and the dining room staff had to muck in and help clean all the plates, pots and pans by hand.

After that task was over he had to get a ladder and clean the nests out of the lights in the dining room.

I think that I've neglected to mention that sparrows flew freely around the dining room and through the kitchens. Sometimes it was like eating in Hyde Park – and I don't remember putting extra mayo on my toast...

('Waiter, there's a fly in my soup!'
'Don't worry sir, the flock of birds circling your head will eat it').

Tuesday 25 August

I had a truly vivid and disgusting dream during the night.

I was standing in a desolate field in the middle of nowhere. It was a freezing cold dawn and the howling wind whined through the bare trees. I was a German dressed in a long, heavy, very warm coat. My name and age were not clear – but I was aware that I was in the middle of a massive war. I felt very confident that my great country would surely be victorious soon. My feeling of power was immense. Looking from side to side, I could see twenty of my comrades standing in a line at regular intervals of a few metres apart.

Like them, I was laughing and brandishing a machine gun.

This was in total contrast to the crowd of people before us. There must have been about three hundred people huddled together, naked and shivering. Some were kneeling, crying, pleading.

Men and women.

Young and old.

Some distant part of my mind comprehended this horrific scene and knew what was going to happen. But my dream persona didn't have a shred of sympathy for their plight. They were Jews. I hated them. They were the root of all problems and had to be disposed of to fulfil the glorious plan of our leader. My superior gave a signal and we started firing our guns into the crowd. The roar of the weapons startled some rooks into flight in the distance but my concentration was on the task in hand.

Some fell immediately. Others shielded the young with their bodies but were soon cut down. A few tried to run but were quickly caught and felled as if in some hideous sport.

Soon the only people standing were my comrades and I, and we walked among the piles of twisted corpses. We could not allow any remaining witnesses to this massacre to survive.

Rain started to fall and I awoke.

I wrote the exact details of this dream down because of its significance to me, which I did not yet understand.

I believe in karma and the notion of 'what goes around comes around'.

The dream seemed so real – as though I had been transported back in time into another person's body. Was this a snapshot of a previous life that I had glimpsed?

Now, here I was, living with Jewish people in their homeland for a year and having a fantastic time. Working voluntarily for them, six days a week, to help support their kibbutz. And all for the equivalent of just one quid a day and as much salad as I could eat. Could there be some concept of justice in the great scheme of things?

Wednesday 26 August

After finishing work, Arthur, Frank, Big Jack and myself caught a bus to Stirot for a mid-week boys' night out.

Over beers and olives we talked about the kibbutz and what each of us thought of it. I said that I'd arrived with a very open mind as to what to expect – but was really enjoying it so far. My work had opened up exciting new dimensions for me in the world of gardening, tractor manoeuvre and sowing the seed.

Arthur explained that after Margarite had left he'd been tempted to follow her but, with hindsight, was glad that he had stayed on. After all he had the rest of his life to return to Brazil. My thoughts exactly. You're only young once. Big Jack supped his Carlsberg, crunched a pretzel and said that he would have gone and lived in a piss-hole in the snow if it had meant escaping from his ex-wife.

French Frank hadn't been in the country for long but he said that it was a relaxing way of life and he could get used to it. We all agreed that the Israeli girls were mighty fine.

Just then a bloke appeared in the bar and started to play a very poor rendition of 'Stairway to Heaven' on his guitar. We showed our appreciation by launching an olive bombardment.

Friday 28 August

Shabbat Shabollocks! (Have a bollocks of a Shabbat!)

I worked in the Noy shed for the whole day repairing broken tools. This was an enjoyable task because I could have as many teas as I wanted and listen to the radio. The little things in life brought so much pleasure now.

Saturday 29 August

Lazy day. Hectic night.

A band came to play on our kibbutz. They set up a stage on the football field in the evening and started practising. Apparently, this event had been advertised and people began arriving from all over the region to watch them.

They weren't too bad but the crowd didn't think much of them because after an hour they wandered over to the pub. It was the busiest I'd seen it so far. Us volunteers had to sneak through the door that led to behind the bar just to get a beer. Luckily the bar staff didn't seem to mind and served us quickly.

I recognised the regular faces but tonight there were a lot of strangers, including volunteers from other kibbutzim further afield. Again, I offered up a prayer of thanks to Boozup (the God of Social Life) that this kibbutz I had randomly chosen had such a popular pub. I overhead Trog moaning to Satsuma. She wasn't too happy: 'There's seven miles of cock in there and I can't even get seven bloody inches!'

Sunday 30 August

The worst and most violent day of my holiday. Big Jack and I had been invited to a party being held on a nearby kibbutz by some volunteers there.

Beer and Bagels for Breakfast

8pm: We got a lift to the kibbutz from one of my KPs, armed with a couple of bottles of cheap vodka and a few beers as our contribution. We searched out the volunteers' accommodation and found our mates, who took us to the bomb shelter where the party had already started. There was a little makeshift bar but we had our own drinks to get started on. The shelter hot and smoky and was crammed with people getting pissed and having a good time. The shelter was very full with young people.

2am: Our mates invited Big Jack and myself back to their rooms for some more drinks as the party was winding down. By this time we were staggering and worse for wear. We got to their rooms and the others went in.

I opened the door of another room and bowled in. There were a couple of English blokes in there who Big Jack knew but I'd never spoken to. I slurred an apology and walked out, pulling the door shut behind me.

WHACK! A fist punched me in the back of my neck and I was eating dirt. I heard shouting and swearing coming from behind me.

Dazed, I managed to get to my feet and saw one of the English blokes (I'll call him Malcolm) standing there and cursing his head off: 'YOU FUCKING WANKER KICKING THE DOOR SHUT! COME ON THEN YOU BASTARD! I'LL 'AVE YOU!'

He was very drunk and I felt the situation was about to worsen.

We started to fight. I wasn't looking for trouble but will always defend myself. I could have been a contender but in my state, my efforts weren't very effective and Malcolm was landing a few good ones on me.

(In the past I had taken some training in karate – but for all the good it was doing I might as well have had a black belt in origami. At this point I could see three of him so was trying to hit the one in the middle.)

People had started to gather to see what the commotion was. My body was so numb with alcohol that I couldn't feel the damage that my face was doing to the other bloke's fists. I was aware of lots of blood that turned out to be mine. Suddenly Big Jack appeared and pulled the other bloke away. Lucky, because Malcolm had just reached down for a broken bottle. (I've since been told he was a psycho who enjoyed fighting and had been kicked off a few kibbutzim because of it).

Big Jack and I went to the dining room phone and called one of the night guards on Naloz. Thirty minutes later I was getting a lift back home.

There was no room for Big Jack and he had to walk the seven kilometres back to Naloz, arriving at about 8am: next morning. Back at Naloz, the doctor put two stitches in my top lip and one over my right eye, which was not pleasant without anaesthetic, but at least I was still drunk.

4am: I took off my bloodstained clothes and slumped into bed. Not surprisingly, sleep was instantaneous.

Monday 31 August

2pm: Big Jack shook me awake and had brought me some soup. It was difficult to consume because my mouth was swollen like a beach ball and hurting like hell, and I had a black eye. My speech was slurred.

Dan had given me a couple of days off after Big Jack explained what happened.

8pm: Dana came to visit and was visibly shocked by the state of my face. 'I am not an animal' I dribbled, 'I am a human being.'

Beer and Bagels for Breakfast

SEPTEMBER

Tuesday 1 September

I stayed in bed all day.

Various people came to visit including some of the soldiers who lived on the kibbutz.

They were good friends of mine and wanted to go on a 'seek and destroy' mission to find Malcolm. I said it wasn't worth it because then his mates would come to Naloz looking for revenge and it would all escalate.

The last thing I wanted was to be the cause of more trouble whilst in Israel and maybe run the risk of being told to leave as an 'undesirable'. As far as I was concerned, if Malcolm was stupid enough to come to our pub then he'd be taught a lesson. Apart from that I just wanted to forget it.

Wednesday 2 September

Back to work. My face was still black and blue but it wasn't an excuse that I could use to skive.

Even though I knew the fight hadn't been my fault, I still felt guilty when the kibbutz members saw me. They had probably heard the reputation of English yobs abroad, and though I knew that wasn't the case with me, it made me feel a bit ashamed as to what some of them might have thought.

Thursday 3 September

Three of the female volunteers that had been at the infamous party came to see me, which was a nice gesture. They wanted to apologise on behalf of Malcolm and said that he'd been thrown off their kibbutz. Apparently he'd even hit one of them in the past. Loony tune.

Friday 4 September

My eighteenth weekend loomed in Israel and I spent it having my stitches removed. Having the ones taken out of my lip was a relief because I was getting tired of picking bits of crusty food off them.

Beer and Bagels for Breakfast

10pm: Skipped the pub and spent the evening at Dana's. (Was it my imagination or did she seem to be more distant these days?)

Saturday 5 September

The lifeguard at the pool told us that it would be closing at the end of the month so we should make the most of it. As I spent most of my spare time in there, it wouldn't really make much difference to me. But I did wonder what there would be to amuse the volunteers in the afternoons once winter had really set in.

One thing was for sure: goodbye swimming, sunbathing, barbecues, sleeping outside, laying sprawled on the grass in a drunken state and gazing up at the stars.

Sunday 6 September

A new volunteer arrived today from the country that I would least have expected – Japan.

His name was very hard to pronounce (it sounded like a cross between a motorbike and somebody sneezing) so he elected to be known as Zero.

His grasp of English was not very good, but a tad better than my understanding of Japanese. Luckily he had brought an English/Japanese dictionary with him to help things along. As you do, I looked up the word 'fuck'. It gave different uses of the word such as 'fuck up', 'fuck around' and 'fuck you'. I also checked 'bastard' and it gave an amusing example: 'This is a bastard of a snowstorm'.

Monday 7 September

Dinner was hilarious because Frank and Zero were trying to hold a conversation but they were both talking about different things. Frank was describing the social scene in Paris while Zero was talking about the affect that drinking saki had on people.

Then Zero tried to teach us some of his language. The tricky concept was that one Japanese word can have three different meanings depending on the tone of your voice as you pronounce it.

Our momentous achievement came when we learnt one single word that meant God/bridge/chopsticks.

Tuesday 8 September

8pm: Every Tuesday, Naloz laid on a trip to a nearby kibbutz that had its own cinema. Big Jack, Arthur, Alien, Trog, Satsuma and myself went to watch 'Dracula'. One annoying aspect of watching a film in an Israeli cinema (for a non-smoker, anyway) is that halfway through the film, the projector stops so that everyone can go outside for a cigarette break. There is no discretion as to when the film is stopped – normally it's when the action is in full flow or when the characters are engaged in a deep and meaningful conversation heavy with tension.

It really bugged me but I suppose it's a boon for people with nicotine cravings or weak bladders.

An electronic beep sounds when the break is over which means you have about ten milliseconds to get back to your seat before the film starts again. Of course people don't make it in time, and so you have human silhouettes crossing in front of you and blocking the screen. Call me a moany old git, but I like to watch films without interruptions.

Wednesday 9 September

Today I learnt all about a horrible feeling – dejection (and rejection).

Dana decided to close our joint love account at the Bank of Heavy Relationships. No longer would I be making deposits and bouncing cheques. In other words she dumped me.

Her reasoning was that we had no future because I would have to return to England eventually, and therefore I couldn't guarantee enough emotional security for her. We were still friends but I must admit to being knocked for six.

Thursday 10 September

Even ploughing failed to lift my mood.

Friday 11 September

I managed to get things in perspective after reading The Jerusalem Post during lunch – there had been a terrorist bomb attack in the north of the country. One youth had been blinded and another had lost a leg.

My problems were absolutely insignificant compared to other peoples' and resolved to give myself a mental kick up the backside.

11pm: Went to the pub, got smashed on vodka and decided to put the last ten days down to a learning experience. From now on life would be a bowl of olives.

Saturday 12 September

Rena told us that the volunteer trip would be the following Wednesday for three days. She would be our driver and we would stay in a cheap hotel for visiting students.

After lunch I went to change some of my sterling into shekels at the kibbutz office. As usual there was a long queue and as usual I was at the end. I hated sitting inside when the sun was blazing down outside.

I spent the rest of the afternoon in the swimming pool bouncing off rubber rings at weird angles.

8pm: I saw Dana at the laundry. Bit awkward... but that's life.

11pm: I saw Dana at the pub. Bit blurred... but that's alcohol.

Sunday 13 September

The dishwasher packed up again today and Dan passed on the message that I had to go and work in the dining room. Whoopy doo. Zero was working there already, and Frank and Arthur had been drafted in, so at least we could have a bit of a laugh. The Voice of Peace was having one of its regular 'nostalgia hours' (which basically meant no talking and end-to-end Sinatra/Presley/Lennon and similar unknowns).

We mimed along as we washed the floor and aurally strolled down a musical memory lane.

Zero said that karaoke bars were very popular in Japan and the sight of drunken businessmen crooning along to an old classic was not uncommon – Frank Sinatra records were apparently the most popular.

September

Monday 14 September

Was thankfully back in the Noy.

I had to trim some trees that were overhanging the animal pens in the children's zoo. That was a good place to hide out because the girl that ran it was really friendly and tea/cakes were always in plentiful supply.

She owned a little dog; the kind that made yapping noises and shivered all the time.

The mutt was dancing around the back legs of the horse that was tied up, making it nervous. I could see what was about to happen but was too late to stop it. The horse kicked out, connected squarely with the dog and it flew across the ground quicker than Sonic the Hedgehog on steroids.

It looked dead. There was no movement and blood was trickling from its mouth.

The girl saw what had happened and came running, nearly slipping arse over tit on some goat shit. She carried her dog into a hut and washed its face with cold water. Five minutes later it regained consciousness and started to shiver again. This time it had a reason I suppose. The dog was checked out by the kibbutz vet and found to only be suffering severe bruising of the mouth.

Tuesday 15 September

I checked sprinklers over by the Russians immigrants' caravans today and the time flew past. All the volunteers were eagerly looking forward to three days in Jerusalem.

Wednesday 16 September

Our party set out from the kibbutz just after breakfast.

We had a lot more space than in the minibus, without the camping and cooking gear that we had to take last time. The journey to Jerusalem took about two hours and the traffic started to get quite heavy on the outskirts. I was quite surprised at the altitude of Jerusalem – I had thought it would be closer to sea level. In the final stages of the drive, we climbed steep roads, which afforded us excellent views over the surrounding hills. Clusters of white houses were clearly visible in the distance and we had ample opportunity to take some photographs as our vehicle laboured up the hill. The height also brought with it a slight drop in temperature compared to what I had been used to. I imagined Jerusalem to be freezing in the winter, and Rena told us that they normally had snow. I began to make mental plans for a Christmas excursion here.

We arrived at our hotel and it was much better than a youth hostel, where it's advisable to share your sleeping bag with your valuables. I bunked with Big Jack, Arthur, Frank and Zero while Rena was in with Trog, Alien and Satsuma. After lunch we set off to explore the New City of Jerusalem.

There was nothing new to see in my opinion. Just shops, restaurants and the highlight – a multi-storey car park. All these sights were part of everyday life in England and so I was a tad disappointed.

Our next stop was to see the Knesset, the Israeli Parliament. To my way of thinking it looked like a modern version of an ancient Greek building, and came across as being very impressive. Near to that was the Israel Museum. As my memories of museums consisted of endless boring school trips around echoing halls containing bones and flint arrows, I must admit to being less than enthusiastic about the prospect of a visit.

I was wrong, it was actually very interesting. We spent the rest of the afternoon there, looking at art collections, a Near Eastern archaeological collection, several important Dead Sea Scrolls, Jewish ritual art, Middle Eastern ethnological exhibits and a sculpture garden.

8pm: Rena decided to stay at the hotel so the volunteers got taxis into town to check out the night's entertainment. We had some drinks in an area that was buzzing with people. It seemed a contradiction to be getting drunk in the world's holiest city... but then I thought of the amount of wine that Jesus and his mates must have got through around these parts.

11pm: We finished the night in an English-style club called The Underground. It was the main after dark hangout for foreign travellers, and there were a lot of Brits and Scandinavians. The club was divided into two sections. The bar was upstairs and the dancefloor downstairs. It was a great place – by the end of the evening, people were unashamedly dancing on the bar.

In the taxi on the way back to our hotel, the driver asked us boys if we wanted to get a prostitute for the night. He drove us down some seedy streets and tried to haggle us a price in Hebrew with an old hag who resembled a bull terrier that's pissed on a nettle. After telling the driver that we weren't going to splash our cash on a back street bunk-up, he drove us to the hotel. He had the cheek to charge us extra fare for the detour!

Thursday 17 September

The Old City.

We went in through the Damascus Gate, which took us into the Muslim Quarter of the Old City. The other three sections were Christian, Jewish and Armenian. The Old City was exactly how I'd imagined Jerusalem to be. Little alleyways leading off in every direction, and bustling crowds of people everywhere. It was nirvana for the souvenir hunter. Shops and stalls were laden with carpets, ornaments of camels and elephants, wooden crosses and 'authentic' holy water, pots and kettles.

The air was heavy with the aroma of mouthwatering smells from the food being sold: bread, meat, schwarma (kebab), falafel and endless varieties of very sweet cakes.

Being in Jerusalem, I decided to be original and buy a wooden cross. A shopkeeper enticed me into his shop and gave me a cup of coffee. This hospitality symbolised the fact that I was expected to buy something in return.

'Where you from?' he enquired.

'England,' I replied.

'Ah English. I have good friend in London!' he beamed.

Call me cynical, but he would probably have had a good friend in the Amazon Jungle if I'd said that was my home.

Anyway, to cut a long story short, I haggled him down from ninety shekels to forty for a wooden cross. I loved bartering – it's always easier if you don't want the thing in the first place; but there's always the danger that they'll call your bluff and agree a price, only to get a bit hot under the scarf if you change your mind.

Having once worked as a share dealer in London, I felt pleased that my razor-sharp business sense hadn't left me. Until, that is, I reflected on the cold fact that I'd just forked out a fiver for a bit of wood that the shopkeeper had probably made for twenty pence. That must have been the most expensive cup of coffee I've ever had.

Beer and Bagels for Breakfast

We negotiated our way through the twisting alleys and found the Western Wall (also known as the Wailing Wall).

It was much smaller than I'd imagined it to be. We passed through a security check before being allowed into the area. The wall was divided into two sections: male and female. After putting on a paper kippa (a little religious hat) we were allowed to go up to the wall. It was customary to write a prayer on a piece of paper and stick it in a crack in the wall, which would then hopefully come true. I wrote a prayer asking to win the Lottery.

After that our group went to the Church of the Holy Sepulchre via the Via Dolorosa. This is supposed to be the last path that Jesus walked on his way to the cross. Uphill all the way, it must have been quite a trek.

I was suspicious about the church because it was meant to contain the site of the crucifixion AND the tomb where Jesus was laid out. As it was quite a small building I couldn't really imagine the cross and the tomb being so close together. In my opinion, it might contain one of the supposed locations, but not both.

We then went to the Temple Mount where the Dome of the Rock is located. This is the famous golden-capped building that is always prominent on holiday programmes.

As its name hints, there is a rock inside. This shrine is sacred to both Muslims and Jews.

To the former, it is the site from which the Prophet Muhammad, founder of Islam, ascended to heaven; to the latter, it is the site at which Abraham (the first patriarch of the Hebrew people) prepared to sacrifice his son Isaac. We went into a small cave under the rock where people were praying.

I felt claustrophobic, so went back outside and collected my smelly Reeboks. There was a little kid hanging around selling post-cards so I bought thirty for one shekel. Who said I couldn't cut a deal?

To round off our Old City tour we went to the Garden of Gethsemane where Jesus was betrayed, and saw the Mount of Olives.

That night we went back into the New City to the Arizona Bar. It was half empty which left me with a bad impression of the place – but it's probably alright when full.

Back at the hotel a group of female students invited Big Jack and myself into their room for a 'cultural exchange'. They were friendly girls. Things got a bit risky when we had to hide in their bathroom because the teacher came to check on them.

Friday 18 September

For the last day of our volunteer trip we visited the Holocaust Museum (Yad Vashem).

Some of the images I saw were terrible, but it was very moving – every visitor to Jerusalem should go there. I thought that it would all be doom and gloom. Instead, the atmosphere was mainly one of curiosity and wanting to be educated about what happened during the Holocaust.

On the way back to the kibbutz we stopped at an old monastery where the monks made their own brand of white wine. Rena bought some bottles for us.

6pm: Back at Naloz we showered, went to dinner, played a drinking game with the potent monastery wine and stumbled to the pub for the remainder of the night. The sophisticated finale of another great volunteer excursion.

Saturday 19 September

There were only two Saturdays to go until the swimming pool shut for the winter, so the volunteers spent the day swimming and sunbathing.

10.30pm: The evening consisted of the usual run-of-the-mill drinking and debauchery.

Sunday 20 September

I acted like a fool at work and got caught out.

As part of their upbringing, the teenagers living on the kibbutz had to work a certain number of days every year in return for a free trip to Greece.

Dan had taken a day off from the Noy and had given me a list of jobs to do. It meant I was in charge of the boy and girl who had been listed to help me do the gardening.

3pm: The kids had worked well so I decided to let them go early.

As we were packing the tools away they spotted the motorised platform that was used to cut tall trees, and started to pester me for a ride on it. I said no because children weren't allowed to operate the heavy machinery.

They kept begging (and after all, the boy had driven a tractor before) so I gave in: 'Alright then. But only in the yard and not too fast.' I started the platform up and manoeuvred it into the centre of the Noy yard.

The boy had a go first, and to my great relief, got the hang of driving it quite quickly. He was on there about five minutes. He came down and the girl jumped onto the platform and started to raise it up while the boy shouted encouragement. Then things started to go not quite according to plan.

I saw Dan walking towards the Noy along a path.

'Quick get down! Dan's coming!' I hissed up at the girl.

She jumped down and left the platform raised a fair bit. As the controls were up there also, I had to quickly shin up the connecting part of the machinery to the platform. There was no time to turn it off and park it so I rolled over to the two date trees by the entrance of the yard.

Dan walked over and asked what I was doing.

'I thought that these two trees needed a quick trim before finishing for the day,' I replied, with my mental fingers crossed.

He thankfully agreed and went into the store to mend some tools. It was typical of him to do a little bit of work even on his day off. I admired that trait but wished that he'd decided not to, just this once!

At least I'd got away with it. Or would have done had fate not meddled.

As I swung the platform around to move it into its parking place, the end smashed into the top of a large pipe sticking out of the ground. I knew that the water inside was pumped under very high pressure but the sight to behold filled me with dread.

Thanks to me, there was now a lovely fountain forty foot high and the beginning of a river running through the yard. I wondered if Dan would notice the extremely loud whooshing noise and the fact that it was artificially raining in the middle of an Israeli summer.

I think the river alerted him. He ran out and gawped.

It goes without saying that I was soaked through, the two kids were laughing their heads off and I felt like a right prat. I hadn't seen such a stony look on Dan's face before. He told me to get the platform out of the way whilst he went to find the manager of the fields who controlled the water supply to the kibbutz and who would be able to turn this section off. The river of water was now eroding the soil at the base of the two trees and the roots were clearly visible. This was a nightmare.

The fountain acted like a beacon and people started to drift along to have a laugh. All I could do was sit and stare at the chaos. Can you imagine an ant's toenail? That's how small I felt.

Ten minutes of humiliation later the water abruptly stopped before Dan and the manager of the fields arrived.

It was a serene scene now. The sky was blue, the birds were singing and we had our own lake where the end of the pipe should have been.

Dan had calmed down. I was mighty relieved. I helped him dig down to the main pipe and we replaced the broken one before filling the hole in. The repair job took about an hour during which time a quarter of the kibbutz was without water. I was covered in mud – and that's what my name will be now, I thought. Dan took a different view: 'Don't worry,' he laughed. 'Everyone breaks a pipe at one time or another.'

I thanked my lucky stars that he could see the funny side.

7pm: Dinner. The other volunteers kept on asking me to 'pass the water'. Ha bloody ha.

Monday 21 September

French Frank attempted to cut Zero's hair with some hair clippers. I could have made a better job of it with the hedge clippers.

Zero wasn't best pleased and Arthur finished the job off properly. With Zero's consent, he even stencilled the word 'ZERO' on the back of his head by varying the clipper guard and length of bristle.

It stood out and Zero pointed to a phrase in his dictionary that roughly translated to 'cool as a penguin's turd'.

At dinner the members stared, but nothing the volunteers got up to really surprised them now.

Tuesday 22 September

Work today was like a spaghetti bolognese. Messy to get through but very enjoyable. It involved my two favourite ingredients: cutting trees and driving the tractor.

Beer and Bagels for Breakfast

After Dan had cut some trees down, I had to drag them around the kibbutz ring road to the dump behind the swimming pool. I could be seen a mile off because the leaves attached to the trees and branches acted like a giant broom, and a massive dust cloud billowed behind me.

Occasionally a hapless car driver would be stuck behind me faced with two options: overtake me at suicidal speed on a blind bend or eat my dust, sucker!

After a few hours' overtime all the necessary trees, branches and the odd geriatric lizard had been dragged to the dump: R.I.P. (Rest In Pieces).

Wednesday 23 September

8pm: The volunteers had a barbecue in The Valley.

We put the word out and told people to bring a bottle but that the food was free.

Guy had kindly given us some steaks and burgers. I never ate boring burgers in England but now they were a luxury to me. We built an excellent fire and made the compulsory punch for when the beer supply got low, consisting of vodka, arak, gin, tequila – and some orange juice for the ladies. (Only kidding, girls...)

Later, we had an 'air guitar' competition. Mere mortals should not have to behold such sights.

Trog won with a wicked 'Come As You Are' by Nirvana and Zero was a close second with a blistering rendition of 'Money For Nothing' by Dire Straits.

A creditable last was Frank with his realistic impression of Jimi Hendrix choking to death on his own vomit (but luckily Alien slapped Frank's back and the offending olive popped out).

Thursday 24 September

6am: I'm not normally sick after a heavy bevy, but this morning my stomach rebelled and I just made it to the toilet in time for a 'Hughey Green'.

Thankfully work wasn't strenuous. I helped Galit and we basically sowed the seed, so nature could grow the seed and then in the future we could prune the seed. See?

Friday 25 September

Fully recovered for the weekend's activities.

The next few days were going to be great because it was the Jewish New Year coming up on September 28 – and that meant special food, days off work and an extra pub night on Monday.

Saturday 26 September

The volunteers resided by the pool for the whole day because it was closing in a few days time until the following summer. As a closing gesture we switched on the sprinkler system and cooled everyone down.

8pm: Laundry time: social mingling place of the universe. I splashed out twenty-five shekels on a rather fetching hooded sweat-shirt in preparation for the coming winter.

11pm: The alcohol flowed freely and Zero was introduced to a new dance concept, to accompany the song 'Creep' by Radiohead. It involved shuffling around the floor very slowly whilst staring down at the ground and holding one's balls. Zero carried it off with style and we bought him a round of drinks for his efforts. This symbolised what it was all about: the mixing of ancient cultures, traditions and trying to get a laugh out of making each other look an idiot.

Monday 28 September

Rosh Hashana (Jewish New Year).

According to certain teachings, the New Year festival 'ushers in the Days of Judgement for all of mankind' but despite its solemnity the festive character is in no way diminished.

7pm: As on Shabbat, the tables in the dining room were arranged in rows. For some reason, every plate had a fish head on it, and some joker had stuck a cigarette in the mouth of one. The evening started with members taking it in turns to say prayers and read out best wishes for the coming new year, followed by a few traditional songs.

It's customary to have bread and apples dipped in honey to symbolise a 'sweet' new year. The menu resembled a dentist's night-mare; delicious substantial food along with cakes and coke. More songs and dances by the members followed the meal and everyone clapped and sung along. Not speaking the lingo, volunteers could only mime the words.

11pm: Free pub. I saw a lot of members who didn't usually attend strutting their stuff and making up for lost time! One old bloke was dancing like a puppet on acid. I made a fool of myself by trying to chat up my kibbutz mum but at least she saw the funny side.

Trog won the volunteer drinking competition. Those Finnish girls must have had hollow legs.

Wednesday 30 September

6am: I woke up and smelt the coffee – but quickly realised it was Big Jack farting on the other side of the room.

It was going to be Yom Kippur the following week, which meant another day off work. It's a great time of year to be a volunteer because there are so many celebrations and commemorations to experience.

The swimming pool closed permanently today, and all the volunteers were all going to miss it

OCTOBER

Thursday 1 October

An intriguing observation as I walked around the kibbutz cutting, chopping and cleaning. Considering the number of dogs that roamed free there was hardly a dollop of canine excrement to be seen. Not that I specifically set out to look for it, you understand, but it struck me as a bit odd and wasn't to be sniffed at.

Since arriving on Naloz all those months ago, I'd taken to walking around the place barefoot. My feet had never been allowed so much air to breathe in their lives and now they resembled a pair of chiropody Chippendales.

The odds were that by now I should have felt the brown stuff squidging between my toes at least once. But nothing. I felt cheated. Not even a dried turd under a toenail.

Friday 2 October

Roughly five months had passed since a naive boy had stumbled through the kibbutz gates – transformed into a lean, mean gardening machine. Basically, I was now a hunk of horticultural hormones.

So, I didn't tell anybody when I got a thorn stuck in my foot. Just put a brave face on it and went straight to the kibbutz nurse. No fuss. No bother.

'NO! NO! NOT THERE!' I shouted as the nurse dug around in my foot using a pair of rusty pliers disinfected with battery acid. (Actually, the pliers weren't quite rusty.)

11pm: Hobbled back to the pub and got a round of beers from the bar. No matter how often the volunteers asked me, I declined to repeat the story of how I'd fought the poisonous snake and stopped it attacking a small child. They could have made a film about it but 'My Left Foot' had already been done.

I glanced over to the other side of the dance floor and noticed that one of the army girls was eyeing me up. As I looked, she suggestively ran her tongue over the bristles on her top lip and twirled her nasal hair around her little finger. Oh well, it had been a while since 'Peter Pecker had picked a pickled pepper'. I sauntered over and started to chat her up in an embarrassingly drunken fashion.

'What's a girl like you doing in a nice place like this?'

(Oh shit; I screwed that one up).

Beer and Bagels for Breakfast

'What's your name? Believe me, darling, once you've had a Noy Boy you'll never look back...'

Ten minutes later we headed back to her room. I must admit to feeling cocky. Or was it her feeling my cocky?

Then things got wild. I experienced the same feeling that a doomed mouse does when a mischievous pussy toys around with it just before eating. Fireworks exploded, trains entered tunnels and old film of large chimneys collapsing flickered backwards.

I felt well chuffed. I'd always thought alcohol caused premature ejaculation.

Saturday 3 October

After lunch the volunteers borrowed the children's zoo tractor and took a ride out into the fields. We packed some beers, a radio, football and a pack of cards. It wasn't exactly chilly, but the heat was not as intense as it had been during the summer. It was the equivalent to a hot July weekend in England.

8pm: Watched a film in the Member's Club. After it finished, Arthur, Big Jack, Frank and myself took a trip into Stirot for a visit to The Shooting Star. We decided to have a break from the kibbutz pub (and I didn't really want to bump into the army girl from the previous night's liaison). I got much drunker than on previous occasions and this nearly got me into serious trouble.

Firstly, I started to act the prat who thinks that he can pull any girl he fancies as though they haven't got a say in the matter. According to Big Jack, I went onto the dance floor and started to gyrate with an Israeli girl even though she was dancing with her rather large boyfriend. He walked off to the side and said something to a few of his mates who looked over. They weren't amused.

Luckily for me, I didn't even notice this because I just toddled off somewhere (to the bar probably), and nothing violent happened to me. It would have been justified if it had, though.

When we left The Shooting Star and walked to The Warehouse, I was swerving along the middle of the road performing the old standard 'look at me I'm pissed therefore immune to being knocked over and killed' routine.

Suddenly a police van came along and I held out my palm to stop it. Big Jack cringed as it pulled up and stopped. I wobbled over to the window and slurred 'Shalom officers' and just walked away.

It must have been my lucky night because the police decided to drive off. I could have found myself down at the station singing those deportation blues. Thinking over this later, I realised that my diary could have ended here and it would have been my own stupid fault.

Sunday 4 October

I worked in the factory today because a couple of the men were away doing their army reserve service. After finishing the compulsory army service at twenty-one, every male has to do an extra month each year. This usually involved routine things such as guarding other kibbutzim.

I must admit to hating the factory work.

I closed my eyes and imagined myself back in England attending my Chess Club and getting down to some real action.

9pm: After watching 'The Simpsons' on TV, there was a new show on the cable channel, 'The Hitcher'. It consisted of 'Twilight Zone' type tales whereby at the end the scruffy hitchhiker of the title would stroll casually onto the screen and utter some fabled words of advice (even though he hadn't been a part of the preceding story). I felt a strong spiritual urge to take heed of this knowledge and base my life around it.

Tonight's story was about a bloke who preyed on lonely women and was eventually deceived himself, resulting in his head being blown clean off his shoulders by a femme fatale's bomb.

The Hitcher was spot on with his ten-second appearance and message: 'Beware – because sometimes the hunter becomes the hunted.'

Like, heavy or what?

Monday 5 October

I decided to clean my room. Like scratching an itch, it had to be done.

Volunteers received free cleaning materials from the shop, including toilet paper and scrubbing pads (any similarity is entirely coincidental).

The black mould in the shower reared up and tried to slither away as I approached, but it was no match for bleach and elbow grease. The mosquito corpses smeared on the wall suffered a similar demise. We had a pet spider living in the corner of the ceiling above the sink and decided not to evict him because he earned his keep by catching little bugs.

Big Jack saw to the dust under the fridge and the beds, whilst I went outside and challenged Trog to a game of 'Catch The Egg'.

This involved throwing an egg at each other and moving further apart after each catch.

Tension, concentration and then I misjudged a catch and lost. There is some scope here for crap puns such as 'having egg on my face' and 'eggcellent game' but I won't stoop so low.

It would be an eggstremely bad yoke.

Tuesday 6 October

My visa was due to expire again in about a month's time. I had heard it was tricky to stay longer than six months so I wasn't sure how to get another one.

There was no way I wanted to return to England yet. I was having a great time and still had quite a bit of money left. I held up my shears, shook them in defiance and swore an oath: 'Mountains may crumble, fires may rage, oceans may boil, but I will never depart these shores until ready!'

If it rained too much, though, I might reconsider.

Wednesday 7 October

Yom Kippur (Day of Atonement), the holiest day of the Jewish calendar. It is a day when sins are confessed and man and God are reconciled. I feel it's only right to admit that, yeah, I do pick my nose and eat it.

Thursday 8 October

The volunteers heard some interesting gossip today from the army lads living on the kibbutz.

Apparently, the lifeguard of the pool had been in trouble with the police in the past, and was now an informant for them. Some of them had invited him to their room several times to have some beers and smoke some dope. The kibbutz members had suspected it but couldn't prove anything. Now that the lifeguard's contract was up, he was free to report back to the police. Consequently, the soldiers had been warned to cease with the blow or face heavy trouble. They didn't realise that at their little gatherings there had been more than one type of grass present.

Friday 9 October

There were about ten kids helping us in the Noy today because we had to collect palm leaves and branches for Sukkot, or the feast of Tabernacles, the following Monday.

Once there was a decent amount on the back, all the kids sat on the edge of the trailer and I drove the tractor to the children's nurseries where the leaves and branches had to be left in piles.

The children were looked after here during the day until their parents collected them at four o'clock.

During the day, they drew pictures, played games, slept, made cakes and went for toddles around the kibbutz with their minders. These jobs went to women on the kibbutz, but often a female volunteer would work here too.

I thought the job looked well cushy but they argued that it can be quite stressful sitting in the sunshine reading stories, gossiping and drinking coke.

4pm: I was surprised to see Dana waiting at my room with one of her dogs, Rotem.

She told me that Rotem would have to be put down unless a home could be found for her. Volunteers weren't allowed to have their own pets because eventually they would have to leave the kibbutz, leaving another stray.

Rotem was a cute dog though and I missed my own back in England, so I agreed to look after her until a permanent home could be found. Big Jack didn't mind having an extra guest in the room.

We made her a dog basket using a Carlsberg box with a blanket inside, and put it in the corner.

The problem was to keep Rotem hidden from the kibbutz vet for the time being, until the heat was off. We could have done porridge for harbouring a fugitive, but they were just wild and crazy times.

10pm: It was drinking games time in the Finnish girls' pad before the pub opened. We'd managed to get six bottles of Shabbat vinegar – sorry – wine, and Frank had a bottle of vodka. Two hours later the public house establishment was open for the enjoyment of its patrons so our motley crew went to get some free drinks. I felt a bit sick and thought that moderation would be sensible – so went easy on the pretzels. I took some back for Rotem who was busily nibbling one of my work boots in frustration at being in solitary confinement.

Saturday 10 October

'That's it baby, lick my feet. You've got a tongue like an epileptic eel – ah, what a toe job! You give great muzzle...'
MUZZLE??
I snapped awake and kicked Rotem off my ankles.
She thought it was a game and started to attack me as I hid under the sheet. I threw a sock onto the huddled shape of Big Jack over the other side of the room and Rotem leapt across the chasm, landing on his back.
'Get off, you little bastard!' he muttered. I opened the door and let the dog out for a piss. At least she hadn't left a puddle on the floor. I love dogs but wouldn't have been too happy at getting out of bed and skating across the floor.

Sunday 11 October

Work in the Noy was now concerned with preparing for the onset of harsh weather during the winter. This meant doing such tasks that would not be worthwhile, or even possible, if it was raining.
The kibbutz sprinkler system had to be checked, even though it wouldn't be needed during the coming months. Dan said the weekly kibbutz newsletter had credited me (along with Dan and Galit) for making the kibbutz look so good. I don't want to blow my own trumpet but that was high praise indeed because volunteers were rarely mentioned in the newsletter for the jobs they did. It was strange to see the squiggles of Hebrew that represented my name. The kibbutz movement had been very clever in choosing the term 'volunteer' as regards to people like myself. If we ever moaned about our lot, or were disappointed about the way things turned out for us, we just had to reflect on that word – volunteer. It said it all.

October

Other volunteers, visiting our pub on a Saturday night, had told me horror stories about the way they got treated. Most said their kibbutz took the attitude that they should be grateful for the salad and cell they got in return for six to eight hours' work a day, six days a week. The one pound a day, equivalent wage, was an added bonus.

Was it just luck that had brought me to a friendly kibbutz like Naloz or was it because I had come with an open mind and willingness to try new experiences?

Monday 12 October

Sukkot (Tabernacles). This is the festival of the harvest and is celebrated for seven days. The concluding eighth day is a separate holiday.

Today the children used the palm leaves and branches to build huts outside their nurseries, and around the kibbutz. These are meant to commemorate the booths that the Israelites resided in after the Exodus.

Tuesday 13 October

The children constructed a camp behind the swimming pool. They were going to live there for three days but it was hardly roughing it because I've never seen a better-equipped camp. They had mattresses, a water boiler, fridge, electric lights, sound system and – yes – a kitchen sink to wash the dishes in. I wanted to ask if the volunteers could move in permanently.

The idea of isolation was lost somewhere along the line because a lot of them kept sneaking off home for showers and to watch TV. Their camp was near where I dumped deas tress, so during the day I made a few detours on the tractor to drop in for a visit and barbecued steak sandwiches.

Wednesday 14 October

Zero received a surprise package sent from his parents. It contained flypaper and a poster of a tiger.

I kicked myself – I knew that I'd forgotten to pack the essentials when leaving home.

Beer and Bagels for Breakfast

Thursday 15 October

My trip to Be'er Sheva.

I caught a bus to the town early because the Bedouin market starts at around six in the morning, and finishes by noon. I was determined to get some cheap presents to take home for my family.

The market consisted of jewellery, cloth, ceramics and rugs. I toyed briefly with the idea of buying my mum something she'd always wanted – a goat. The idea of trying to smuggle it through customs under my coat put me off. So I decided to purchase a carved wooden elephant instead. I bought a necklace for my sister and a pot for my dad (because he's always complaining that he hasn't got one to piss in).

After a few more hours, I went to the shopping mall and found a quaint eatery called Pizza Hut to have lunch in. There was a distinct lack of haggle here as the prices were plainly fixed on the wall.

Friday 16 October

Being a Piscean, I tend to have a very generous and giving nature, and I find it hard to say no.

This, subsequently, was the cause of a gruesome murder on the kibbutz that could so easily have been avoided.

The memory will always haunt me...

During my morning tea break I parked the tractor behind the dining room and joined the workers there for some grub.

I got talking to Trog who worked in the kitchens, and she asked if it was possible to have a quick spin on the tractor before continuing work. As she couldn't even drive a car, I was a bit wary of agreeing to her request. Then I thought that, like me, she'd come to Israel to try new things – and who was I to stand in her (fourteen stone) way? Gleefully revving up the engine, she started to reverse the tractor in a shuddering way. Her foot slipped off the clutch and the tractor shot backwards.

The trailer behind slammed into a wall and we stalled. Once my teeth had stopped chattering I told her to take things a tad more gently. We set off again and headed for the kibbutz office. Things were going smoothly and Trog was doing quite well. I relaxed.

Suddenly, directly in our path, I spotted the unluckiest lizard in the world taking a morning stroll in the sunshine. Trog was busy concentrating on avoiding parked cars and small children and hadn't spotted the hapless reptile.

The lizard saw us bearing down and tried to make a run for it. He scuttled across the road one way, and then back again.

I was shouting evasive manoeuvres: 'Go left... no right... left... quick right...' For one hopeful moment the odds looked favourable and then fate dealt a cruel blow.

The lizard stumbled over a pebble and I caught a fleeting glimpse of wide frightened eyes (swivelling in different directions) as he went under the large front wheel.

Nothing could survive that. I jumped down to have a look.

Miraculously he was still alive, but had nothing to celebrate because his insides were now on the outside. One eye swivelled towards me and pleaded for mercy. I put cardboard over his head and squashed it in a humane way, before throwing the corpse into the bushes.

Even though I hadn't run him over, I felt guilty imagining the lizard widow and orphans waiting back home in the nest, crying over his last words: 'I'm just popping out for a few flies, darling. Won't be long.'

11pm: Trog and I drowned our sorrows in the pub and made a toast to the late lizard.

We requested The Kinks song 'You Really Got Me' in his memory.

Saturday 17 October

I had my hair ruined by the kibbutz barber and paid ten shekels for the privilege. It was my own fault because I couldn't wait until the following day to catch a bus into Stirot to have it done properly. Even though I resembled a monk my polite English upbringing came to the fore: 'Thank you, it looks great. Here's a tip.'

Checking the coast was clear, I hurried back to The Valley where Arthur did me a favour and cut it short all over to even it up. It was the shortest it had ever been.

I slicked it back with hair gel and had a photo taken with a toy gun and a knife because I looked like an assassin.

8pm: The family of an army friend of ours lived in Be'er Sheva and the guy (called Alon) knew the town well. He hired a minibus and took us all to the university there. The student union bar was open on a Saturday night serving cheap drinks.

Beer and Bagels for Breakfast

10pm: We went to an Indian restaurant. It was heaven because missed having a regular curry and was experiencing Balti withdrawal symptoms.

11pm: We spent the rest of the night at a place called Ha-Simta that was very popular. Throughout my year in Israel, this was one of the best nights I had.

It paid off making friends on the kibbutz because it created opportunities to do things that you might miss if you weren't prepared to join in. I could honestly say that by now I knew most people on the kibbutz and had some very good friends. Considering a volunteer works, eats and (occasionally) sleeps with the people that live there every day, it isn't really that difficult.

Sunday 18 October

Dan helped me to secure a platform onto the lifting arms at the rear of the tractor. Then he borrowed a forklift truck and put a barrel of old crude oil and diesel fuel onto the platform. He made a hole in the side of the barrel and attached a plastic tap and a long length of hose.

I had to find the stumps of trees that had been cut down and use the oil to burn them.

3.30pm: Mission accomplished. I was covered in a greasy mixture of oil and diesel but satisfied. As I was chugging slowly back to the Noy shed along one of the paths, I heard a splashing sound coming from behind me.

I looked around with dread.

The tap had fallen out of the side of the barrel and I was leaving a merry trail of oil along one of the main pathways. It looked a bit crude. This was made worse by the fact that the children's nurseries were nearby and it wasn't very healthy to toddle home through an oil slick.

I jumped down from my seat and rolled the barrel around so that the hole was pointing upwards. Then I forced the tap back in and went to get some buckets of sand.

It took me five trips laden down with heavy buckets of sand to cover the oil and soak it up.

7pm: Dinner was memorable.

The volunteers who smoked usually put their cigarette ends into any bowls of uneaten soup that had gone cold. There was one such appetising bowl of vegetable soup – complete with seven ciga-rette butts jostling with the croutons for space.

We added coffee, ash, sugar, salt, tomato sauce, sweeteners, orange juice and some chilli paste for that extra touch of 'joie de vivre'.

French Frank was willing to earn some easy money. The evening's entertainment was the volunteers giving Frank five shekels each for him to eat it all. I'd always thought the French took pleasure in gastronomic delights, but was proved wrong by the look on Frank's face as he forced the fag soup down.

Afterwards, he complained that there was too much salt.

Monday 19 October

We had a holiday to celebrate the end of Sukkot. I borrowed the key to the pub and taped some of the CDs and albums. My music collection had vastly improved since arriving on Naloz. Through borrowing people's music, I had a stack of tapes containing every-thing imaginable.

In the afternoon, we lazed around in The Valley drinking beers and then went to have a pool competition in the games room. The volunteers had a key because we used it the room the most and kept it relatively clean. The TV was linked to the kibbutz video. Often the members would set up a mock TV station broadcasting from a studio above the dining room. This included phone-in competitions and all were encouraged to play a part.

Tuesday 20 October

Zero and I were working in the turkey sheds for the next four days. Forty thousand baby chicks were scheduled to arrive on Thursday.

Thursday 22 October

With the accommodation completed for the chicks it was time to sort out the food. I had a chocolate bar and Zero had some ice cream. Once that snack was over, two bucket-loads of feed were put into each pen, but not in a haphazard, devil-may-care sort of way. Oh no.

Beer and Bagels for Breakfast

The piles of food had to be strictly placed under the heating lamps so that the chicks could eat and keep warm at the same time. Pampered or what? Once that was done, the gas heaters were switched on so that the temperature of the shed would be just right for the chicks' living conditions.

They were arriving later on in the evening, so Zero and I had some extra work to look forward to. I knew what to expect from my time off-loading the young chickens earlier in the year. The boss told me to boil some water and add three bags of sugar to it to make a very sweet mixture. This was to give the chicks extra nourishment, strength and horrendous dental fillings later on in life.

7.30pm: A few of the other volunteers were asked to help with the imminent arrival, so Arthur, Frank and Big Jack joined Zero and myself in grabbing a quick sandwich before heading over to the darkened turkey sheds. The routine was the same as when the chickens arrived. There was one difference; no talking was allowed because it stressed out the chicks.

Apparently, for the first few hours after the chicks are hatched anything they see is labelled 'mum'. Therefore once unloaded into their pens they were not to be disturbed until the following day.

We carried them in trays, turned them upside down and the chicks tumbled out and started to walk around exploring their new home. There were some dead ones, which were placed in buckets to be burnt the following day.

9pm: The job over, we emerged blinking into the headlights of the lorry, sweating and smelling of roast turkey. There then followed a mad scramble to be first in the showers.

Friday 23 October

Zero had booked a day off so I was working by myself.

My last day with the turkeys comprised of making sure their food was topped up and rescuing any that had fallen into the water bottles. If I found any panting and looking dehydrated there was a set routine to be followed.

This involved picking the chick up, swirling its head in the water to cool it down, and then forcing its beak into the water so it could drink about six sips at a time. There were quite a few in this condition as they congregated around the heaters and lay with their eyes shut. (They would eventually be oven-ready turkeys, but the majority already looked oven-done.) Those members who had worked with the turkeys for years were practical and efficient about it. Only the strongest chicks could be reared (and sold for a profit) and therefore any that were too weak to survive, or already in the process of dying, had to be burnt along with the corpses in order to prevent the spread of disease or the interest of rats.

Even though I understood this, it still seemed cruel to be roasted alive, so I made a decision.

I cringed whilst doing it, but any living chicks that had to go 'in the bucket' had their small necks broken quickly by me. In my opinion, it seemed more humane than burning them. I was happy to try out new jobs but this was one I didn't relish having to do again.

Saturday 24 October

We invented a dance phenomenon that came to be widely known as The Ace of Base, and will go down in Israeli popular culture as the movement to be seen indulging in at the trendiest of clubs...

'Do The Ace, and get outta my face!' would be the shout going out.

To be honest, much of the credit has to go to the hip Swedish pop combo of the same name, for giving us the idea. Hey guys... if you're reading – respect is due.

The birth of the movement began while we were watching MTV. The volunteers were supping beers, and commenting on how similar all the music videos were. Just then 'The Sign' came on by Ace of Base.

I can tell you: I saw the sign and it opened up my eyes.

This video was different... radical... some would even say dangerous.

While the song played, the band members struck poses and held them without moving. They resembled statues of perfection. The full range of vulnerable emotions was laid bare, and the volunteers couldn't help but be moved. There was the 'longing gaze into the distance'; the 'sulky, smouldering look at the camera'; the 'arms fully outstretched in a needful display of passion'; and (the classic) 'crouch with chin resting on hand whilst contemplating romantic dilemma with furrowed brow'. All volunteers felt compelled to lay down bottles and practice.

Beer and Bagels for Breakfast

After a mass debate we settled on the final concept that would
be introduced later that night in the pub. Thus:

once any Ace of Base song was played, we would stroll at our
leisure to the dance floor and strike the first motionless pose. Every
participant had to choose a different one. After ten seconds, another pose was selected and held for a further ten seconds. And so on,
for the duration of the song.

1am: The dance floor was packed and there was a good crowd.

We were getting edgy. Not a single Ace of Base song had been
played, so Arthur pushed through to the DJ and requested 'Don't
Turn Around'. The first melodic bars came on, and we strolled
leisurely onto the floor. There was no hurry. We took our time.
Maximum effect.

Our first poses were struck with perfection. People were turning around to look at us.

We gazed straight ahead, deliberately oblivious. Then some of
the dancers started to jostle us and make faces as close as they
could, trying to put us off. Who did they think they were dealing
with – amateurs?

This was the start of The Ace movement. We had to demonstrate
it professionally.

Out of the corner of my eye, I saw a bloke pushing Frank's face
and laughing.

Would Frank buckle under the pressure?

Like a true Ace of Base pro, he chose the only option open to
him and went into an emergency crouch. The timing was immaculate and coincided with the designated ten-second change of pose
that the rest of us were smoothly effecting. After that we all had
our own private little battles of people bumping, tickling and pushing us – but we came through our first Ace of Base unscathed.

Three minutes later (which seemed stretched to three hours)
the song faded out and we calmly strolled off, cool and composed.

We even got a little applause.

Sunday 25 October

After a brief taste of heady fame, it was back to earth with a
bump today – nearly literally.

Some of the telephone wires had fallen down near the kibbutz
gate, and Dan asked me to help him fix them back up again. Rather

than use a ladder, Dan had the next best thing – a bulldozer! He borrowed it from the garage and trundled up to the first telephone pole.

Dan elevated me to the dizzy heights and I affixed the first wire to the pole then gave him the thumbs-up signal to move slowly along.

With hindsight, I suppose it wasn't Dan's fault that he pushed the wrong lever. The shovel started to tip down and my horizontal position rapidly became vertical. I grabbed hold of the large metal prongs on the edge, and hung on for dear life as my feet scrabbled for a foothold. Dan couldn't hear me shouting because the roar of the engine was too loud. Luckily my guardian angel made me drop the hammer and it fell in front of Dan, accompanied by a hail of nails. That should alert my boss to his assistant's precarious predicament.

He looked up and quickly pushed what he thought was the right lever back again. The shovel began to shake and it felt like clinging onto a skyscraper during an earthquake. My balls were clacking together like castanets.

Just as my vision began to blur the shaking ceased and the shovel righted itself. Dan lowered me to the ground. I wobbled around picking up the hammer and nails whilst he familiarised himself with the correct levers to finish the job (and not finish me off).

Monday 26 October

5am: I worked in the almonds today. The lines of almond trees stretched as far into the distance as I could see, and it was a good job that a lot of people worked here because of all that had to be done. There was also a group of Arab workers employed on a daily basis, working for peanuts (not almond nuts).

The system that the kibbutz used to collect the almonds was ingenious in its speed and efficiency; a tractor dragged a very large polythene sheet along the ground, which was spread around the base of a tree. Another tractor with a special set of pincers on the front grabbed the base of the tree and shook all the almonds off onto the sheet.

This was repeated along the line of trees until there was a huge pile of almonds on the sheet. A lorry was driven up that had a special hydraulic lifting arm, which attached to a corner of the sheet holding the pile of almonds.

As the arm was raised, a large 'hammock' was formed, swung over to the top of a trailer, at which point I jumped onto the trailer and, unfastening two corners of the sheet, emptied the almonds in. Once the trailer was full I drove the tractor back to the kibbutz.

Dug between the factory and the garage was a deep pit with a metal grille across it. I had to reverse the trailer over the grille and park it securely. Easier said than done because the back wheels had to go as near to the edge as possible so that the almond load poured squarely into the pit. The grille acted like a large sieve and stopped any branches, rocks and other debris from falling in. When the pit was eventually full with almonds, a lorry would drive down a gradient into the pit and collect them for market.

1pm: After eating, we went on working until we finished at about 6pm: To finish up, we lubricated our parched and dusty throats with some cold beers, slapped each other on the back and sang some rugby songs.

Tuesday 27 October

A bit of a downer: the volunteers had to leave The Valley and move back to our original accommodation. More Americans were coming to do their army service, and so the kibbutz needed the extra rooms because they would be staying for a few years. (Plus the fact that their rich parents didn't want their precious little lambs to rough it with us barbarians.)

I borrowed the Noy tractor and after four round trips carting all our stuff, including the luxury fridge, extra tables, chairs and a few kettles we were settled.

Rena dropped by and gave us some heaters for the coming winter.

Big Jack and I managed to procure a white, furry carpet that was no doubt extremely fashionable in the psychedelic Seventies. This would put an end to bare feet on a cold stone floor and give Rotem a comfortable base to lie on. So I had the dog at my feet, the fire to sit by – all I needed now was a pipe to smoke and a good woman by my side.

Wednesday 28 October

I booked the following Wednesday off with Dan because I had to visit Ashkelon again to sort my visa out. This would be tricky because technically I had been a resident for longer than six months. My fate rested with the dragon at the Interior Ministry and what sort of mood she happened to be in.

I remembered speaking to a volunteer from a nearby kibbutz who was nearly in tears because the woman had refused to renew her visa. Despite the girl explaining that she was in a serious relationship with an Israeli member and wanted to stay for another six months, it hadn't cut any ice with the woman who just repeated: 'I'm sorry, those are the rules. You have to leave Israel.' I didn't want to hear those words because I was enjoying myself too much.

So I ran blubbing to my kibbutz mum who told me that she'd have a word with the Secretary of the Kibbutz to see what plan of action could be followed.

That night I slept peacefully until Rotem started yapping to be let out. It was too late anyway as she'd already pissed on the new carpet.

Thursday 29 October

6am: On my way to breakfast I dropped the carpet off at the laundry to have a thorough cleaning.

Sorted out some warmer working clothes before the temperature dropped too dramatically and they started disappearing.

In the dining room I munched my toast, boiled eggs and salad and fantasised about bacon, sausages, beans, mushrooms and grilled tomatoes.

I was just beginning to dribble when my kibbutz mum came in. She told me that the Secretary of the Kibbutz wanted to see Rena and myself on Sunday to discuss my visa application. I found a window in my diary and confirmed the appointment.

Friday 30 October

I cut the grass for the last time this summer. Using only a hand-pushed lawnmower, I worked around the play areas in the children's nurseries.

Beer and Bagels for Breakfast

These were always good places to work because the army girls would invite me in to test out their cakes, have coffee, gossip about old Mrs Scratchett at number eight, etc.

Dan had given me a list of old people on the kibbutz whose lawns he wanted me to cut. More coffee and cakes, but less chat because only a rare few of them could speak English. By now, I could hold a very simple conversation in Hebrew, and it was interesting to see if the older members could understand me.

There were a few misunderstandings, but intelligent hand signals got the main message across when my grasp of the language failed me. For example: I was trying to explain the fascinating subject of the bourgeoisie influences inherent in Post-Impressionist sociological Siamese art of the sixth century to an old lady, when she nodded and gave me two sugars in my tea.

8pm: Shabbat dinner. As was the norm, everybody except the volunteers seemed determined to get through their meal as quickly as possible, and leave. The only reason we could see for this was because the members had nice homes to return to with televisions, stereos, computers, fridges flowing with food. We had a board game with pieces missing and some chocolate spread to fight over!

There were consolations though. I got two bottles of wine for our fridge and some schnitzels for Rotem.

4am: Bit of an embarrassing Ace of Base towards the closing stages of the pub, but everyone was pissed so it didn't really matter too much. 'All That She Wants' was playing and Arthur, Frank and myself were holding the pose successfully.

A couple of Israeli girls that we knew walked over and started to dance provocatively in front of us, testing our resolve (and the tightness of our jeans).

It would take more than that to put a true Acer off his calling in life. The exact same thought must have crossed their mischievous minds, because suddenly they unzipped our flies and pulled our jeans around our ankles.

I'd had my kecks dropped in more intimate settings but never in the middle of a public disco.

I could see Frank and Arthur enduring the same torture and caught a glimpse of my boxer shorts reflected in the wall-mirror. A grinning Garfield the Cat seemed to be mocking me.

Enough was enough when I felt my boxers being frantically tugged, so I employed that trusty escape clause and went into an 'emergency crouch with pout into space'. Bare legs were OK but bare bums would be too much. After all, my nether regions weren't tanned.

Saturday 31 October

Cleaning day. Rena supplied the materials, and the volunteers mucked in and washed the accommodation blocks right through. Spiders were evicted, showers were scrubbed and Rotem was hidden in a wardrobe.

11pm: Things nearly went off in the pub (and I don't mean my jeans).

The Americans staying on the kibbutz were a great bunch and got on very well with the volunteers. It should be said, though, that every barrel has its rotten apple – and this one was called Montgomery Jnr. He was a rich little shit who looked upon volunteers as the scum of the earth. His parents had sent over a colour television for his room amongst other homely things, but Montgomery Jnr wasn't satisfied. He wanted our fridge.

Ever since we'd moved out of The Valley to allow him to move in, Montgomery Jnr had whinged about his living conditions, and how we hadn't left anything behind. He seemed to think he owned the place and had a chip on his shoulder the size of Ayers Rock.

Montgomery Jnr was getting pissed as the evening went on, airing his views about how unfair life was ad nauseam. We could see him sneering at the volunteer corner in the pub and Big Jack, in particular, was getting wound up by his attitude. Montgomery Jnr started to air his grievances to Big Jack after bumping into him outside when returning from a piss in the bushes.

I could see them arguing and you didn't have to be an expert in body language to guess they weren't swapping stamps. From the look on his face, Montgomery Jnr had realised he'd picked the wrong person to have a go at.

A few bystanders had gathered around to shouts of: 'It's not worth it...walk away!' 'It's only the beer talking!'

Big Jack was just preparing to batter Montgomery Jnr when the little Yankee wanker muttered: 'OK man, point taken. Cool it. Keep the damn fridge!'

He skulked off, Big Jack calmed down and I knew how close Montgomery Jnr had come to the prospect of sucking his food through a straw. This was all over the fact that he wanted to prove himself superior to volunteers in some small way. Petty? I don't think so. We worked just as hard as little prats like that and had the God-given right to keep our candy and sodas cool too.

NOVEMBER

Sunday 1 November

2pm: A high-level meeting took place between Rena, the Secretary of the Kibbutz and myself.

Rena put forward a good case on my behalf about living on the kibbutz for another six months. My kibbutz mum had already given me a great reference and apparently Dan had put in a good word for me.

The fact that not many volunteers stayed for the winter went in my favour – a lot came just for the hot summer months and then returned home for the start of term at university. But, set against that was the realistic point that there were not a lot of jobs to put volunteers in during the winter.

The Secretary asked me if I minded the possibility of doing other jobs when things were a bit slow in the Noy. I agreed to this because it seemed as though I moved around a fair bit anyway.

Now that the Secretary had agreed I could stay, the next task was to convince the people that really mattered – the Israeli authorities. Another suggestion was put to me which I readily agreed to, and a letter was written (the contents of which I am not allowed to mention here). I never expected the kibbutz to give me this level of backing. After all, I was only a glorified tourist.

When the meeting was over, we all promised to do lunch sometime and I went back to work, relieved that my holiday was not over.

9pm: Some of the young Israelis booked out a couple of minibuses and invited us to a nearby beach, where we built a fire, lounged around on blankets, listening to Israeli music, drinking beer and chatting. A week ago there was the real possibility that this could have been my last party in Israel. I stretched out on my blanket, gazed up at the night sky and counted my lucky stars.

Monday 2 November

Rena called a volunteer meeting in the TV room and made a welcome announcement. The kibbutz members appreciated the fact that one of the obvious reasons we had chosen to travel was to see new countries. Because of that, they were allowing us fifteen free days off to go to... Egypt!

The trip would replace the regular scheduled volunteer trip, and we would have to cover the costs ourselves. We could leave most of our belongings on the kibbutz and the trip wouldn't constitute a break in the time that we had registered on the kibbutz. That meant once we'd returned, we could go back to our jobs, did not need another AIDS test and would not be treated like new volunteers who have to begin on the dishwasher.

My mind was made up: I was gonna go and party with the Pharaohs and swing with the Sphinx.

Tuesday 3 November

I saw my first snake in Israel. Not being an expert on reptiles – the last one I'd had dealings with was unintentionally pulped by Trog – I kept my distance. It was roughly a foot long, dark in colour and kept flicking it's tongue at me. I ignored all the old don't worry...it's probably more scared of you myths and bloody legged it.

Wednesday 4 November

I enjoyed a few more hours in bed before struggling up and departing for battle in Ashkelon.

This time my confidence was boosted by the secret weapon I had in the shape of a letter from the kibbutz Secretary. I jauntily sauntered into the Interior Ministry building, took my numbered ticket and sat down to wait.

The wheels of the Israeli bureaucratic system seemed to be well oiled for a change, and I entered the visa office only three hours after arriving.

There she was: the Devil in human form...She Who Walks Backwards...Mrs Beelzebub. I sat in front of her whilst she carried on marking forms for a few more minutes. Making me wait. Playing the power game.

I glanced up at the clock as the minutes audibly ticked by.

Eventually she peered across at me, and I felt my eyebrows (yes, they had grown back) frost over.

My passport floated across the desk and opened itself before her. She flicked through it as the sweat prickled on my forehead. I see you have been here for six months already child, she hissed. Time to go...

I think not! The letter was thrust towards her, and she shrank back. Picking it up carefully and scrutinising it she made Tut Tut noises (in Hebrew).

Then a shaft of light speared through the window behind her, illuminating the letter. Her expression was grim, I knew that victory was mine. Brandishing a metal stamp, my passport was marked with another three months.

Three months? Not six? I looked at her and she grinned: See you in February, maggot!

This battle had been won, the war was to follow. I would cross that bridge when the time came.

Thursday 5 November

Those that wanted to spend time in Egypt had to tell Rena today. The Egyptian posse comprised of Arthur, Frank, Trog, Alien and Satsuma and myself. Zero had decided to stay on the kibbutz because he wanted to spend as much time as possible improving his English, and Big Jack didn't have enough money for the trip.

Rena took us to a town called Ashdod to have an injection immunising us against malaria. She took us into the hospital and we waited outside the nurse's room. The pervading smell of disinfectant and echoes of squeaky plimsolls on the shiny floor seems to be a feature of all hospitals. I just wanted to get in, do the jab and get out.

Just then the nurse appeared, took down our particulars and asked who wanted to go first. Alien was always keen for a prick in any way, shape or form and volunteered to lead the way.

Once back at Naloz, we trooped along to the nurse, who gave us with a fifteen-day supply of pills. Two had to be taken every day to stop us getting the squirts and another one had to be taken before, during and after the trip as a back-up against malaria. The main advice she gave us was not to drink the water and to keep our mouths shut when taking a shower.

Friday 6 November

It was Big Jack's birthday. The volunteers decided to deliberately keep it low-key and throw a surprise party before the pub opened. He knew that we knew, but at breakfast he couldn't resist dropping a few subtle hints such as: I can't believe it... fucking thirty-seven today!

We just muttered a communal: Oh right. Happy birthday, and disappeared off to our various jobs.

When the kibbutz shop opened I ducked in and bought the three C's (chocolates, cake and coke) which were debited to the volunteers joint account. I also bought a tacky birthday card that played the tune Congratulations in a tinny, microchip sort of fashion when opened. (You can't buy class but I tried.)

4pm: I finished in the Noy and went back to the volunteersí blocks. Big Jack was sitting outside with Arthur and Frank drinking beers. It was obvious that he'd had a few. About ten by this stage...

What a fucking birthday. I'm miles from me family and the only present I've got to show for it is a fucking flea bite from Rotem.

He was trying to joke, but you could see Big Jack was a bit gutted about the apparent lethargy on our part to celebrate his birthday. Since he'd arrived on the kibbutz this was the most pissed I'd seen him so far (and he could hold his drink).

Don't worry mate, I said. Here's a card signed by all of us.

Cheers everyone, he replied, and started to sing along to the tinkling tune of Congratulations. This was a sorry sight – but we didn't want to give the game away about the party later. We had a few beers on the porch and then trooped over to the dining room for the Shabbat meal. A girl played a Hebrew song on a clarinet, and Big Jack started to clap along a bit too loudly, but at least he had cheered up. A good thing too, because some of the Yanks were going to be at the party and the combination of a drunken, bitter Big Jack and a whinging little shit like Montgomery Jnr. didn't bear thinking about.

After the meal had finished, Big Jack, Arthur and myself sat and tried to win the Last Table Award.

We normally did this when there was nothing else for us to do, and it just simply involved us trying to be the last people to leave the dining room. There was some stiff competition tonight from a family and their guests so we finished off a bottle of wine. The delay was good because it gave Trog and Satsuma time to return to the volunteers blocks and get the fire going and the food organised.

We eventually went back to the rooms where the Yanks and some of our Israeli mates were waiting. We told Big Jack the purpose of the party and he was over the moon. As there wasn't much choice of presents to buy in the shop, the volunteers gave him a bottle of vodka, some shaving stuff and a packet of chewing gum.

The drink had taken maximum effect by now and he was slurring the usual statements that are forgotten when sober: Cheers...fucking great...come here, you're me best mate...nah straight up...I had no idea you old wanka...!

It was a great boozing session rounded off with free drinks in the pub and a bop.

Saturday 7 November

I think it was that great statesman JFK that once proclaimed: Christ, what a headache! – and I could sympathise this morning. My hangover had bells on it. I opened my eyes and found myself sprawled out on a chair in the TV room with absolutely no recollection of how I'd got there. The last thing imprinted on my blurred memory was being bundled about on the dance floor to Ain't No Doubt by Jimmy Nail.

With that cringeworthy thought lingering, I pulled my jeans back on, spat the dead spider out of my mouth and walked back to my room. With hindsight, it would have been polite to have knocked, but my thumping hangover was spurring me on to find some Aspro Clear. I walked in and was greeted with the sight of Big Jack having a shag.

Oops! Sorry mate! I exclaimed, and quickly went back out, wondering who he'd managed to pull.

(It turned out to be the young aunt of a mutual friend who was visiting the kibbutz.)

Anyway, it was about time for lunch so I went to the dining room and had some mud coffee. Big Jack eventually turned up and I apologised again for interrupting his rhythm. He told me that, coincidentally, I had come in as he was coming.

7pm: Feeling recovered, I had some food. It was always the same on Saturday nights – eggs and chicken soup left over from Shabbat. It was so salty, we nicknamed it Dead Sea Soup.

11pm: The last pub night before Egypt. I joined Frank, Arthur and Zero in a last Ace of Base before the trip. Some of the Israelis even joined in. The movement was getting so popular everyone would probably be doing it by the year 2059.

Beer and Bagels for Breakfast

Sunday 8 November

After a long, hard day of working in the Noy, there's nothing that a volunteer likes better than to relax on his favourite old settee, switch on the telly and watch an entertaining programme such as Home & Away.

Home & Away? I couldn't believe it – the dreaded theme tune began and the words drifted from the set: You know we belong together, you and I forever and ever...

It's a reasonable assumption that by travelling thousands of miles to the Middle East there might be a slim possibility of escaping the curse of the S.O.F.A. (Soap Opera From Australia).

But no. There is a market for them in Israel even though the plots are far behind the English episodes – not that I watch them, you understand. Honest guv.

Anyway, I didn't really have much to do, so having been a media student in the past, I decided to analyse Home & Away and try to work out the dominant ideologies involved through a process of selection, omission and representation in a mediating sort of way. (In other words, I was going to watch it and get hooked like most sad people end up doing.)

Monday 9 November

A tough day at work before the holiday. There was long driveway leading from the kibbutz gate to the main road, and on one side was a row of young trees. They had grown to a reasonable height, but the prevailing wind from across the open fields had made them lean over. I had to try and straighten the trees up and tie them with strong string so they could grow upwards, and not sideways.

After breakfast, I went and collected the Noy moped from the garage, and burnt off in a squeal of rubber through the kibbutz. This job was trickier than I thought it would be. First, I had to roll an old oil drum next to the tree and try to stand and balance on it as best I could on the sloping ground, whilst swatting away the flies buzzing around my ears. Then, I had to select a stake that was roughly the same height as the tree, and hammer it into the ground next to the trunk (which was only a few inches wide at this age).

Dan had thoughtfully sharpened the other end into a rough point so they went into the ground quite easily after a few hefty thumps. The most important thing was to ensure that they were firmly set because the tree would rely on this to keep it upright.

I used a special type of knotted loop to tie the tree to the stake. Dan had shown me what to do; it ensured the trunk would still grow thicker, but still be held firmly in place. It prevented the string from cutting into the soft bark as the tree matured and therefore stopped any rotting or disease in the future.

I felt a warm glow from the fact that for a change I was helping nurture trees, rather than hacking their limbs off. Long after I'd been gone, future visitors to the kibbutz would be able to turn to each other with a smile as they passed along the driveway, and remark: My, don't those trees look damn straight. I'm privileged to have seen them.

1pm: Dan let me finish early so that I could go and sort my stuff out for Egypt. Taking The Jerusalem Post back to my room I read an article about a bloke that had been caught by customs attempting to smuggle some drugs into the country under his foreskin.

Two thoughts struck me.

He was obviously not Jewish. And where would he have hidden crack cocaine?

Tuesday 10 November

Day One.
1am: I swear even my dog Rotem had a tear in her eye as I turned and bid farewell.

Whoa, hang on! Slight deja vu there for a moment as the Naloz volunteer group set off on the first stage of our trip to Egypt. Rena gave us a lift to the bus station in Be'er Sheva to catch the daily 2am bus bound for Eilat, where we would get our Egyptian visas at the consulate. We boarded the bus and settled in for the four hour ride.

The bus stopped once on the way to pick up more passengers. There were no more empty seats available, so the unlucky newcomers were forced to sit on their bags in the aisles.

6am: I could just see the sparkling lights of Eilat coming into view and woke up Satsuma next to me who'd been fast asleep catching flies.

The coast arced in a bay, with plenty of hotels along the beachfront. The architects and planners of Eilat must have filled every available space, because the buildings, shops and beach area were concentrated into a small stretch of land. Jordan was clearly visible on the far side of the bay.

Arthur, Trog, Alien and Frank had woken up and were busy rubbing the sleep from their eyes and blinking out the windows.

We arrived at the bus station and the heat washed over us as we stepped off our cool, air-conditioned vehicle. It was like being gently blown with a hairdryer and that's no exaggeration. Even on the kibbutz it hadn't been this warm so early in the morning. I could only imagine what the climate would be like at midday.

A girl came over and asked if we were looking for a good hostel, and gave us a leaflet advertising Fawlty Towers and we decided to give it a try. After all, with a name like that and the promise of a free beer, how could we refuse? After ten minutes of hiking uphill with our rucksacks, the sweat was flowing freely so we stopped at a supermarket to buy some bottled water. Lots of it.

The heat was very dry rather than humid. I knew from school biology lessons that the human body is made up of eighty percent water. During the walk to the hostel I must have lost at least half that. We found the Fawlty Towers and booked a bed each in a dormitory that would sleep eight.

8am: We changed into our swimming clothes and went to explore after breakfast in a snack bar consisting of falafel (deep-fried ground balls made of chick-pea), kebabs and orange juice. I hadn't eaten since the last kibbutz evening dinner and was absolutely ravenous. The sun shimmered on the pavements, and for once I had my shades on for reasons other than posing. The beach was crowded, mainly with young Israelis, and the sand was so hot I had to keep my shoes on. Yet, across the road, there was a new hotel being built by workers who looked to be Arabs. They were wearing jeans, jumpers and cloths under their hardhats, completely covering their heads. I couldn't understand how they could work in such heat dressed like that.

We picked a spot near a bar that was on the beach, and laid our towels out. We took it in turns to look after our stuff while the other volunteers went to swim.

The Red Sea was crystal-clear and beautifully warm. There were two wooden platforms situated a bit further out and Arthur, Frank and myself swam out to them. People were diving and somersaulting backwards off them, which we also tried. The platforms were pyramid-shaped so the higher you dared to go, the further you had to jump outwards otherwise your head and wooden surface might connect in a most unpleasant way. I just about managed to dive down and touch the sandy floor but my ears were popping like mad. Arthur and Frank both retrieved a stone to prove they'd also reached the bottom.

Occasionally, a plane would come in to land at the airport, which was not far from where we were staying. It was an impressive sight watching a plane flying in so low over a beach, only just seeming to clear the hotel roofs

After all the volunteers had enjoyed a long swim we decided to have a go on the Banana. This was a long, yellow inflatable plastic lilo that got pulled along behind a speedboat.

There was space for eight passengers at a time, and as we all wanted to be on the same ride, the bloke who ran it said that we could leave our stuff in his office and it would be looked after.

Donning our life jackets, we climbed on and grabbed hold of the plastic handles. The speedboat roared away, there was a sharp tug and we were off and running. The Banana bucked and bounced over the waves while we held on for dear life. It was very fast and we thought it a great achievement to have stayed seated for so long.

But the speedboat driver could have had us off any time he chose – which he promptly did.

Slowing down slightly, and then suddenly steering the speedboat in a very tight curve at a fast rate of knots, the Banana tipped sideways and we all smacked into the water, and at that speed, it certainly hurt!

Because I was seated at the back, I flew a little further through the air and landed on Alien's head. Just as she was coming up for air my weight took her under again and she was coughing and spluttering. Everybody recovered and bobbed around in the sea whilst we waited for the speedboat to circle around and collect us for another go.

The ride lasted about fifteen minutes and is highly recommended (especially if you crave the taste of sea water).

Bad news awaited us. Only one shower was working in the hostel because a pipe was being repaired (the owner hadn't mentioned that little detail when we'd booked a bed).

8pm: Spruced up and clean, the volunteers set off to check out the night's activities. We found a bar just a few streets from our hostel called the Peace Cafe. They served cheap beers and some food, and the music was good. We were too knackered to walk any further as we'd been up since the early hours, so we decided to hang out there for the evening.

Some of the other drinkers said that the Peace Cafe was a good place to find casual work if we were interested, but our agenda was already set.

There was one bloke in the Peace Cafe who was pissed as a fart and falling about on the floor mumbling about something or other. Eventually, he fell asleep slumped across one of the tables.

A few of his mates got a razor and started to shave off his hair – which was funny but well out of order. He woke up, and not surprisingly wasn't too chuffed with his new Kojak. After some harsh words and curses a drunken fight broke out. I grabbed my bottle of Carlsberg, and joined the other volunteers under a table where we carried on drinking.

Above us, in the Peace Cafe, the violent brawl continued.

Wednesday 11 November

Day Two.
9am: We walked into the town to get some passport photos taken for the Egyptian visa. The beach was already crowded and people were swimming, parasailing and water-skiing. The consulate wasn't easy to find. I'd assumed it would be in the centre of town, but it was tucked away in a residential area and we had to walk through many winding alleys before spying the Egyptian flag poking over the houses. We filled out an application form, paid our forty shekels and left our passports and photos to be collected later in the afternoon.

There were a few hours to kill so we went to the beach and wandered along the promenade to the marina. This was the social hub of Eilat, with numerous restaurants, snack bars, pubs and clubs.

1pm: We collected our visas from the Egyptian consulate and were relieved to discover that there hadn't been any problems in issuing them. It would have been nasty to be refused entry after so much anticipation.

All this walking through the hot streets had taken its toll, and we headed for the cool sea to try water-skiing. It cost fifty shekels for only fifteen minutes, which I thought was expensive, but then everything cost more in Eilat. It was definitely the place to have a good time and not count the pennies. After instructions on how to lean back on the skis and ride the waves, we set off. I started off sitting in the water holding onto the rope that was attached to a speedboat. As we moved up, I rose up and found myself in a standing position. Not too bad for a first attempt.

But I began to get a bit flash, jumping across the waves. Then, whilst trying to spot the other volunteers on the beach, I totally lost it and sprawled into the sea on my face, which is when I had a moment of pure and utter shock. I've always had a phobia about floating alone miles out at sea without being able to see what's swimming below me.

While waiting for the speedboat to circle back, I happened to glance down into the water at my legs – and saw what I thought was a grey shark coming up towards me. My stomach flipped. The Red Sea is notorious for its sharks and poisonous snakes and I didn't want to have a run in with either. But, I'd forgotten that I was wearing grey skis, and as I paddled my feet, they had reared up towards me from below.

9pm: A walk along the promenade, looking at cheap jewellery for sale, and artists drawing cartoon caricatures of tourists. Satsuma wanted a likeness done, but the artist insisted on some danger money up front. We then found a bar, Yatush Barosh, and we stayed there for a few hours, drinking expensive beers and watching the hip young things pass by. Eilat was a place for people -watching.

At around midnight we breezed over the bridge to the other side of the marina and decided to try out a club called Sheba's, which had an English DJ playing, a laser show, and lots of beautiful Israeli girls.

Ten out of ten for fun... nil points for air quality.

Thursday 12 November

Day Three.
9am: We bid a not-so-fond farewell to the Fawlty Towers hostel and walked down into town.

Eilat was obviously geared towards tourists coming for a few days and splashing lots of cash having a great time. It didn't pretend to be anything else. Some of the volunteers thought it to be a tacky town, but I loved the relaxed atmosphere, heat and beaches.

We caught a bus from Eilat to Taba, on the Sinai border. The Sinai Peninsula is strictly part of Egypt, although its ownership has been disputed by Israel, which even led to wars between the two countries in the Sixties and Seventies. Thankfully relations between the two countries have improved considerably since then. The journey only lasted about ten minutes and we were treated to a great view of the Red Sea as we drove alongside the coast. Then through passport control, we paid our forty shekels departure tax, and walked through no man's land before Egyptian immigration. We were allowed in after some form filling, passport stamping and a thorough check of our rucksacks in the security building. As I left this building, I peeped round the corner and took some photos of the checkpoint for my scrapbook. I was careful not to be seen, because there were Egyptian soldiers, and I wasn't sure if photos were allowed. Our passports were checked again as they didn't take any chances with illegal immigration and we had another long walk to the customs building. At the money-changing booth, I had to hand over twenty Egyptian pounds to pay a border tax. It was a bit of a rip-off, having to pay to leave Israel, and pay to enter Egypt.

Safely within Egypt, we needed to find transportation to Dahab, an old hippy hangout along the coast, and we had the choice of two old taxis on the other side of the road. When the drivers saw us coming, they started arguing with each other in Arabic, and trying to tempt us into their own personal car. We quickly discovered that, as in parts of Israel, haggling was the name of the game here. I was getting quite convincing in the art of pretending to lose interest in doing business and walking away.

Eventually, through a diplomatic mix of hand signals and gentle arguing poor we agreed a fare with one of the drivers and he strapped our worldly belongings on the roof of his car.

The journey took a few hours, and we saw Bedouins camping off in the distance, and I wondered how they could live in such isolation. The route took us along the gulf of Aqaba, and along to Dahab, which basically consisted of various camps of tents, camels and stray cats strung along the beach, with the Red Sea just fifty metres away.

The heat was intense but the cool breeze blowing steadily from the sea helped a lot.

We walked along the shore and started to search for a camp where we could stay overnight, as we planned to move on the following day. They were all quite similar, but after a lot of deliberation (the tossing of a spare shekel), we decided to try a place called the Fighting Kangaroo Oasis.

It was only four Egyptian pounds a day, which was cheap – but you got exactly what you paid for. The rooms were basically a concrete hut covered with a thatched roof. We only had two things inside – a thin mattress on the floor to sleep on and a single candle. I would never complain about the kibbutz rooms again!

That was all we needed though. A clean place to sleep and dump our stuff while we lived in the camp.

The communal washing facilities were in a courtyard nearby, and I went off to take a shower. I took along my own emergency toilet roll as I'd heard from other travellers in Eilat that it was very rare to find a scrap anywhere here.

Inside the cubicle there was a round hole in the ground. I walked back out and naively asked someone where the toilets were. He informed me that I'd just come out of it, and could he borrow some toilet paper after I'd finished?

Rumour had it that this wasn't exactly the most hygienic part of the world to be in, but the state of the little boy's room defied belief. I strongly hoped that the anti-trots tablets we were taking daily would do their job properly.

I slid back inside trap number three, and after checking for scorpions, carefully did the business – but didn't bother to pull the chain. There wasn't one.

The showers were quite clean but the water felt really weird. It's hard to describe, but it had a greasy sensation to it. Heeding the kibbutz nurse's words of wisdom, I kept my mouth clamped firmly shut throughout and breathed through my nose. When all the other volunteers had sampled the delights of the toilets and showers we went off to explore Dahab.

A few minutes after strolling along, a guy walked over to us and openly offered a big plastic bag full of hash for twenty Egyptian pounds. He didn't seem to care if anyone was watching him.

Now, I've never pretended to be an expert on the street value of drugs, but even I knew that this was a bargain. As there were only about three places to buy alcohol in Dahab, Frank, Arthur and myself chipped in and bought the bag of blow.

Beer and Bagels for Breakfast

There were numerous restaurants in the Bedouin village and we stopped at one to get some food in anticipation of the munchies. Instead of chairs and tables, the floor was divided into square sections filled with cushions and rugs to lounge on. A few people lazed around puffing pot playing backgammon and listening to reggae music.

Never before, or since, have I experienced such a relaxed, laid-back oasis as Dahab. If the three most important hobbies in your life are smoking weed, sunbathing and listening to Bob Marley while time stands still then head for this part of the Sinai. You won't be disappointed. We ordered some food, lay on the rugs and watched the ocean.

I had a succulent steak that was so big I couldn't finish it, so I gave the rest to the stray cats. Hours drifted by before Arthur, Frank and I headed back to our hut. It was starting to get dark so we lit the candle, and lounged around smoking. As there happened to be gaps in the wall, I'd expected to get eaten alive by mosquitoes but there didn't seem to be any. Maybe we were lucky or they didn't like the sea breeze.

We drifted off to find the girls and decided to visit a recommended dive called the Black Prince Disco.

A truck took us there for free and fortunately it was one of the few places that sold beer. It soon filled up with an unlikely mix of Arabs, Israelis and European travellers. There were also some volunteers from other kibbutzim who were on their way to Egypt.

They said that they'd only planned to stay in Dahab for five days but had been there for two weeks already. I could understand how easy it was just to forget everything and stay for much longer. It was unbelievably cheap to live in the camp, the food was very tasty and the constant background accompaniment of reggae and Pink Floyd suited me fine. We left the Black Prince Disco just as it was getting light.

Friday 13 November

Day Four.

3pm: I emerged from the hut and went for a swim in the sea to wake myself up properly. (These early rises were a killer.)

Surprise, surprise. We all decided to hang around in Dahab for another day. It was a beautiful place.

An old kibbutz tower

The Valley

I didn't really want to go home

A typical volunteer decoration

Swim and admire the beautiful surroundings

The various settlements along the Red Sea in Dahab

The basic accommodation in Dahab

Sunrise over Mount Sinai

Looking towards Gaza from the kibbutz perimeter

A pyramid on the edge of Cairo

Naloz was technically in the Negez Desert

A bird's-eye view of Naloz (similar to living in a park)

Cutting the grass was no longer a chore

A little light reading

Our bomb shelter during the Gulf War

The landscape surrounding Naloz

While Frank and Arthur tucked into the bag of hash, I went with the Finnish girls to have a camel ride.

The small saddles on the camels were definitely not designed for the male gender. There was a raised point at the front that was meant to act as a handle so both your legs could dangle over one side or the other. I couldn't get the hang of this and sat on the saddle facing forwards with one leg on either side.

I was rocking backwards and forwards in the saddle trying desperately to prevent my packet from colliding with the handle on the front at every stride. It was a bruising ride. The girls had tears of laughter at my tears of pain.

We finished the excursion into the desert and I hobbled into a restaurant for a relaxing recovery stretched out on one of the cushions.

After having some lasagne and pancakes I fell asleep in the restaurant for a few hours and awoke when it got dark. We spent the rest of the night at the Black Prince Disco. All of us except Satsuma, who was superstitious about going out on Friday 13th. She stayed in her hut and made hand-shadows of witches and ghosties by the light of a flickering candle.

Saturday 14 November

Day Five.
Yeah alright. We'll definitely leave Dahab tomorrow.

Sunday 15 November

Day Six.
We struggled out of our sleeping bags at the unearthly hour of 10am and had a last swim in the Red Sea. After showering, pissing in the hole in the public convenience and bartering a price with a taxi driver we headed inland towards Mount Sinai.

Dahab faded into the distance behind us. An everlasting, hazy memory of a top place to stay for a few days/weeks/years.

The taxi drivers didn't rush for anything. As we chugged along, I saw a bus full of passengers that had stopped by the side of the road. Must have a flat tyre or something. No, the bus had pulled over for a more urgent reason.

Beer and Bagels for Breakfast

As we drove by, we were greeted with the sight of the bus driver performing the quaint, age-old custom commonly known as having a shit at the side of the road. I don't know what his passengers thought, but could just imagine the reaction if a London bus driver stopped in the middle of Piccadilly Circus for a swift dump.

We reached the vicinity of St Catherineís Monastery at the base of Mount Sinai, and the taxi driver dropped us in the main square. We told the guy at the bus stand that we planned to spend the night at the top of Mount Sinai. He said that for ten Egyptian pounds we could deposit the bulk of our stuff under lock and key. That seemed reasonable, so we picked one bag, filled it with extra clothes, water, snacks money and took turns carrying it up the mountain. We carried our own sleeping bags.

There were two routes to the summit: a long, gentle path or a quicker, steeper one which consisted mostly of large steps cut into the rock. We went for the longer route as we had time on our side.

It was hot work, so we stopped for a breather every twenty minutes or so. In some places the stones were loose, and I slipped a few times trying to cut corners. As we reached the halfway point after about ninety minutes we spotted a tiny hut further along the path. There was an Arab guy inside selling coffee, tea and snacks. This was the most isolated shop I'd ever encountered. It was a welcome respite from the heat, as there was just enough shade for us to crowd under and have a very sweet cup of mint tea. As we climbed higher, the path got much steeper, adding to our weariness. After another hour the path ended and was replaced by stone steps for the final section of the climb to the summit. This was the hardest stage because it happened to be my turn to carry the bag, and my legs began to wobble.

I could see Frank struggling in front of me and I had Trog deep-breathing in my ear from behind.

Finally, we cleared the last ridge. I stand corrected from my earlier statement. There was an even more isolated shop up on the top of Mount Sinai. We bought some hot drinks and plonked our sleeping bags down in a line on the floor, staking the Naloz volunteer territory, while we watched more weary climbers appear and set up their camps. From where we were based, we could see the mountains of Saudi Arabia, Africa, the Gulf of Aqaba and the Red Sea. It was one of the most beautiful views I've ever seen, bathed in a deep red sunset.

As the sun disappeared, the temperature plummeted and we had to put on our spare clothes and get into our sleeping bags. It was bloody freezing up there. The man running the shop was making a mint out of travellers buying hot tea and coffee.

We huddled together and chatted until we grew tired, and then settled down for the night. Arthur and myself drew the short straws because we were the bookends on either side of the group, so we each had one cold side. We had a hard bed of stone that night, and I had to use my trainers as a pillow. So, I lay there on my Reeboks and gazed up at a myriad of stars. Mount Sinai's altitude and the cold air made for an extremely clear sky, and once my eyes grew accustomed to the darkness, I could see far into the depths of space. We were literally sleeping in a billion-star hotel.

Monday 16 November

Day Seven.

5am: It had been too cold to sleep, and I had dozed and shivered through the night, but I was awake to see the sun rise over the mountains. Everyone was already awake, clutching hot drinks in one hand, with cameras poised in the other, ready to catch the first few rays for posterity.

I, however, was more concerned with my posterior, which was decidedly numb after a hard night on the rocks. To give it some exercise, I climbed out of the sleeping bag and over to the shop to get breakfast for the troops. Juggling six cups of mint tea, I picked my way back to our makeshift camp and posed for a few sunrise photographs. After about an hour, we began the long trek down, this time taking the steeper, but quicker route. It took us just under two hours to arrive panting at the bottom – respect is definitely due to the main man Moses, who didn't have the help of the carved steps.

Our next stop according to the rough itinerary we had agreed on at the Kibbutz was St Catherine's Monastery, located at the foot of the mountain, built at the site of the Burning Bush. The Chapel of the Burning Bush had a strict no shoes policy, because apparently the roots of the bush extended underneath the floor, and it was considered disrespectful to walk on the plant.

The Burning Bush was covered, I suppose, to prevent keen gardeners from taking a cutting and growing their own version. As a Noy volunteer, it was like going to the ultimate garden centre to see the most important plant in history.

There were so many icons and holy places in the country it was hard to believe that they could all be authentic. I wasn't really convinced that the shrub before me had actually been on fire whilst issuing orders to Moses.

I'll give St Catherine's Monastery top marks for creating a reverent atmosphere – but as for the manners of visiting American pensioners: must try harder.

We collected our rucksacks from storage and because there wasn't a bus to Cairo for another few hours, we agreed to take a taxi. After a quick haggle, we knocked the original price in half, and bundled in for the six hour journey to Cairo. The drive was monotonous and I fell asleep, catching up on the previous night's lack of Z's.

4pm: Alien woke me up and I massaged my cramped legs. We were crossing the Suez Canal, so leaving the Sinai Peninsula, and arriving in Egypt proper – Land of the Pharoahs!

7pm: Eventually, we made it through the heavy Cairo traffic and the taxi dropped us off in Ramses Square, by the train station. The first step to finding accommodation for the night was a perilous and frightening one, not for the faint-hearted crossing the road. Three lanes of traffic moving in both directions, with cars overtaking in every single lane. The Egyptian driver did not favour their indicators and horns were the accepted substitute. There was no way of predicting which lane they would opt for, especially as it was dark, and most of the drivers hadn't turned their headlights on.

Obviously the traffic flow wasn't going to cease and allow us to walk across, so the only thing to do was to wait for a gap and then quickly run to the middle of a lane. So you're standing there whilst cars and buses whistle past a few inches on either side raising the hairs on your neck.

I've never seen a road system like it.

Arthur took his life in his hands and made it to the central reservation after only three pauses in the process. He was choking on exhaust fumes, pausing to gather his courage before attempting the final three lanes. The rest of us followed suit, running like rabbits.

None of us had a clue where we were going, and we had no map, but we figured we must be pretty central, because of the main station nearby, so we decided to split into two groups to find a room. Frank and the girls stayed with the luggage, while Arthur and myself went to search for rooms. We soon stumbled upon a couple of dirt cheap hostels that were also dirty.

Quite a few little children and beggars spotted us and could see that we were strangers from outta town and they followed us, hands outstretched, saying Baksheesh. I presumed that they wanted money, but I soon found out that the word also applied to tipping. Tips varied from one Egyptian pound (politeness) to five Egyptian pounds (a job well done, mate). I gave a few notes away to ease my conscience... and because the English equivalent amounted to a minuscule sum anyway.

Arthur spotted a reasonable-looking hotel down a narrow street. An old man was at reception, busy reading a newspaper.

Er, excuse me. Hello.

Ello.

How much are the rooms please?

Two stars. Very clean. I speak English.

Right. So, how much?

Showers and clean beds. You like Egypt?

Yeah it's nice. Money? Ten, twenty...?

Five pounds one person. Sign your name and pay pounds.

What a result. This was either the cheapest hotel in the world or the Egyptians dealt in funny money! I was effectively paying an English quid or two for a bed, shower and a good night's kip.

Arthur remained in the hotel chatting to the old guy whilst I went and found the other volunteers. Following the trail of bread-crumbs that I'd dropped earlier it wasn't too much trouble. I shared with Arthur; Trog shared with Alien; Frank tried to act surprised that he was sharing with Satsuma. (We all knew that they'd been shagging for ages.) I opened the shutters and being on the sixth floor the view wasn't bad. Looking onto the hustle and bustle of Cairo, it was exactly how I'd imagined. The sound of the hooting traffic mingled with an Imam's call to prayer in Arabic, emanating from a personal address system somewhere.

The exotic mood was broken by the moaning and groaning coming from Frank and Satsuma's room.

9pm: There was a tiny restaurant in the hotel and we had a filling meal of rice, chicken, vegetables, soup, bread and potatoes.

Beer and Bagels for Breakfast

After we'd finished the old guy invited us have tea with him on the roof patio. The night was really warm and the old guy didn't charge us for the tea. He explained: You, guests in my hotel. You drink tea with me please.

When we ran out of sugar the old guy sent his young son to another hotel down the street to get some. When the boy returned he asked for some baksheesh, but the old guy told us not to give him any. Egyptian hospitality amazed me.

After an hour of drinking mint tea we thanked the old guy and set off to explore Cairo.

A few of the Egyptian men in the streets not only blatantly eyed up the girls...but Frank, Arthur and myself as well! I was glad we were in a group. I wouldn't fancy getting lost in some of the dark alleys we cut through.

Back at the hotel, I switched on the fan and crashed out to the lullaby of a thousand car horns.

Tuesday 17 November

Day Eight.

The sounds of wailing and horns hooting woke me up and the Cairo cacophony enveloped me.

9am: First things first. Visitors to Egypt have to register their passports with the authorities within seven days of arrival, so we set off for the passport office near the Egyptian Museum. The Cairo Metro amazed me; the stations were clean and the trains ran through every five minutes without fail. It was a quick way to cut across the city and avoid the lethal busy roads.

After registering and making ourselves legal at the passport office, we joined the long queue outside the Egyptian Museum. Taxi drivers kept on hassling to see if we wanted to go anywhere. I found the most effective way of showing no interest was to point a fore-finger in the air and waggle it from side to side.

The inside of the museum was similar to a pyramid. There were various floors, corridors and separate rooms within rooms. The exhibition halls held jewellery, weapons, wooden artefacts. People with sensitive eyes should wear shades in some rooms to protect against the glaring amount of gold on show.

The treasures from Tutankhamun's tomb were obviously very popular, and there was a queue of people just for this one room alone. When I finally got to see the Mask of Tutankhamun in a glass case I was surprised at how small it was in real life, and then I realised that it was made for a boy's head.

2pm: After lunch we were accosted by a friendly taxi driver who said that he would be our personal driver for the afternoon for a very cheap price. Sure enough, it was only a few Egyptian pounds – but we didn't realise he had an ulterior motive.

After telling him that we wanted to visit the pyramids, he persuaded us to stop at a factory and showroom that produced papyrus paintings.

I've always liked art and thought that some of the paintings were really excellent, but too pricey for us budget travellers. I would have bought some if the prices had been lower but the owner refused to haggle them down saying that the value was good already. Funnily enough, the owner happened to be the taxi driver's brother-in-law; a strange coincidence I don't think, and a scam pulled on many unsuspecting tourists.

After that we visited a perfume shop on the next stage of the Taxi Driver's Commission From Relatives Tour. Now I understood why his fare had been so cheap, but we didn't mind as we were being taken off the beaten track. After a short demonstration and a cup of tea by the shop's owner (brother of taxi driver), Trog and Alien bought some perfume. Then the owner asked us to leave a comment in his visitors book for future customers to read.

Once the taxi driver had got some business out of us, we headed towards the pyramids along the main road heading for Giza. I was surprised at how close the pyramids were to the main city. I had thought they would be miles out.

But no. One minute you're driving along a busy road in Cairo, the next there's a bloody great pyramid staring you in the face. Television pictures and photographs cannot do them any justice – you can't grasp the scale, or the work involved to build them, unless they are dwarfing you as your car speeds towards Giza.

We arrived at the site and paid our driver half his fare, before arranging a time for him to meet us.

We wandered around in the heat taking photos, not quite believing that these were the real pyramids – that we could actually reach out and touch them. I wanted to take a photo of some old women riding along on donkeys but they wouldn't let me unless I coughed up baksheesh...so I declined.

Beer and Bagels for Breakfast

This was a day of surprises. To me, the Sphinx looked very small indeed and parts of its face had crumbled away. Pictures had not done it justice. Taking a deep breath of fresh air, we crawled through some passages inside the Pyramid of Cheops. This is no good for people with claustrophobia.

Eventually, we emerged into the light and decided to hire horses as the camels were too slow (and painful). We found an Arab kid, probably far more streetwise than we gave him credit for. His father hired out horses to tourists and we struck a deal with him (which included a bit of baksheesh for his son who had introduced us).

Arthur didn't like horses so he opted for a donkey whilst the rest of us mounted our steeds. They seemed to be in prime condition and well fed. One thing was for sure: they hated being tied up and once the two Arabs had led the way out of the street, we were after them at a gallop. Arthur was after them at a trot.

The owner had told us to pull on the reins if we wanted to slow down, and shout an Arabic word that apparently meant halt horse. Mine must have been deaf because it didn't pay any attention and was hell-bent on winning the 3.30 at Cairo. I love speed and galloping through the desert was exhilarating.

One of my lasting memories of the whole year away was riding around the pyramids at sunset.

While the volunteers were having a race I glanced around and could see Arthur trotting along in the distance on his little donkey, trying to keep up. It was a really funny sight and once our horses had decided to stop for a breather there was a chance for him to catch us up.

That was good for me because my camera had packed up in the heat, so Arthur agreed to take some photos for me and send them on in the future. It was just my luck. Here we were at the Seventh Wonder of the World and my bloody Pentax had gone on strike.

We were very surprised to see that our taxi driver mate had turned up as we hadn't really expected him to. He drove us back to the hotel just as the sound and light show began at the pyramids. Other travellers we had chatted to told us not to bother with that spectacle as it was vastly overrated. Before we left his cab, the taxi driver asked us to sign a book with a greeting, thank you or a funny comment.

Great service, from one former cab driver to another! John.

That evening we painted the town red at a club called Atlas that played Arabic dance music. We figured that after all the European stuff we'd heard in Israel, it was time for a change.

Wednesday 18 November

Day Nine.

After some breakfast washed down with Alka Seltzer we went to the train station in Ramses Square to book six tickets to Luxor.

Chaos reigned supreme. At first we queued in the wrong section which was women only. When we finally got to the ticket window the bloke told us to shuffle over to the next line. Of course then we had to start at the end, so to speak. People were blatantly pushing in front of us, so we followed their lead and moved further up to the window. The only objections were in Arabic so we couldn't understand them.

Finally, we managed to purchase the cheapest tickets available (third class) for the evening train to Luxor, which left us some time to amuse ourselves.

First, we caught a bus, which meant literally running alongside one heading in the right direction and picking a good time to leap aboard. Frank horribly mistimed his jump and ended up sprawled at the side of the road. He was really fortunate not to end up under the wheels of the hooting car behind. He quickly got to his feet and ran to catch our bus up.

We soon arrived in Old Cairo and performed an immaculate formation jump from the moving bus. We didn't have a clue where the proper stops were because the buses in this crazy country seemed to pull over whenever they felt like it.

I wanted to get a few presents for the folks back home other than the My Friend Went To Egypt And All I Got Was This Lousy T-Shirt variety of gift. We wandered into a market similar to the one I'd visited in Be'er Sheva.

They were selling different spices and foods and the aroma was amazing making my mouth water... until I passed an old lady cooking something in a frying pan at the side of a path. The food smelt really tempting – a tasty meat of some kind. I glanced down into the sizzling frying pan and saw that she was cooking little chicks. Disgusting.

We ambled along, taking our time having a good look around the market. I wanted to buy some papyruses for my family and myself. I purchased ten cheap ones at an Egyptian quid apiece from a street urchin.

While we were walking, two Arab students came and offered to buy us lunch in return for a small favour. All they asked was that we chatted to them so they could practice their English. We sat outside a cafe, drinking juice made from crushed sugar cane (sweet? – I could feel cavities opening up as I drank) and eating sandwiches whilst having a pleasant chinwag. Their English was very good, and as promised, they picked up the bill. None of us had ever been paid with food to talk before. I don't think the students could believe their luck because Alien just didn't stop yabbering on. An hour later we made our way back to the hotel to freshen up and check out.

7pm: As we waited for our train to pull in, lots of people were praying on mats in a designated area of the platform that had been sectioned off. The only praying I'd witnessed previously in London were frustrated commuters muttering: Please God, let my train be on time.

8pm: After checking with some Tourist Police that we were boarding the correct train for Luxor, our group filed through the carriages searching for the third class compartments. The aisles were very narrow and fellow passengers tutted as our rucksacks bounced along their shoulders. We bumped into a guard and told him that we would be staying on the train until Luxor. He told us the journey took roughly thirteen hours and that we could travel in a sleeper compartment if we wished.

Fantastic – our own travelling bedroom! Privacy and luxury!

Wrong. It should be remembered, reader, that a Third Class ticket in Egypt is a different concept to a similar one in a modernised society.

The guard led us along a connecting passageway that had a separate room next to it with no seats. The dividing wall had nothing covering the spaces where the windows normally go. The toilet was in the adjoining compartment – a round hole cut in the floor of the train. We laid our sleeping bags on the floor and put our rucksacks in the furthest corner, so if anyone tried to steal them as we slept they would have to tiptoe over us first.

As it happened, we didn't get much sleep because most of the time was spent watching the scenery go by and playing cards. Our valuables were inside our sleeping bags for safekeeping, and we made sure one of us looked after the stuff if the others went for a walk along the train.

Throughout the night a guy came along selling tea, bottles of coke and snacks which was a welcome diversion.

When things got a bit slow there was always the opportunity to amuse ourselves by dropping things through the hole in the floor, and trying to break the record for the longest-distance piss along the track. Arthur won that with a memorable two-mile piddle.

Thursday 19 November

Day Ten.

6am: I rolled onto my side and blinked my eyes fully open in surprise. There were about twenty kids crammed in the passageway watching us and whispering. It was unnerving feeling like freaks in a cage with people coming to stare: If you don't eat your greens, Abdul, this is what you'll grow up to be like...

We sat in our sleeping bags staring back at the kids and making faces at them. A few of them laughed and ran off down the train whilst some older ones asked us if we had any spare cigarettes. A Tourist Policeman chased them off. He told us not to give them anything, especially not baksheesh. We got up, washed our faces with bottled water and Frank went to find the guy who sold the teas.

The scenery outside the train was like an amazing moving picture. According to my map we were travelling through the Arabian Desert but it looked very green and lush to me. This was the Egypt that I'd really come to see: concealed away from the beaten tourist track.

We slowly moved past wooden huts and villages complete with children leading donkeys, and old women carrying buckets and bags. The evident poverty in this part of the country made me wonder what went through their minds when the train passed, carrying rich, well-fed tourists waving and taking photos. At one point the train stopped at a signal and a group of Egyptian teenagers started asking us to throw them some cigarettes or baksheesh. Arthur chucked five cheap Israeli fags and a few bars of chocolate, causing a mad scramble in the dust.

10am: Arrived in Luxor. The minute we left the train station we were hit by offers for cheap hotel rooms. The people were extreme-

Beer and Bagels for Breakfast

ly approachable, but we obviously represented giant walking wallets. We decided to find our own place as we knew it was a buyer's market, and cheaper accommodation would be available.

There was a kalishe (horse and carriage) parked on the opposite side of the square, which we hired and the driver took us to the central part of the town. He dropped us off in a busy street, but we couldn't tell which part of Luxor we were in. He assured us with great gusto that it was Middle! Middle! so we paid his fare and palmed him a few extra pounds in baksheesh.

After hunting around, we finally found a bargain hotel for only one Egyptian pound per person per night! This was the ultimate in budget travel with bearable living conditions. Clean, crisp sheets, a hygienic shower, large fan on the ceiling and clean, crisp toilet paper (no rationing in sight). The only condition was that we all had to share the same room. With six beds it was slightly cramped, but what the hell – all friends together! (And for the same price as an English newspaper, tabloid at that, I could put up with Alien's toe sticking in my ear.)

The owner said that for a fee his brother (surprise, surprise) would take us on a tour of the temples. He spoke good English and assured us that we wouldn't get ripped off. It sounded a reasonable offer. We also booked a tour to the Valley of the Kings for the following day. The price was twenty-five Egyptian pounds each, including the ferry crossing over the River Nile, donkey transport and lunch at a restaurant run by another relative of the hotel owner. In Egypt it's not a case of what you know... but who you know. (Failing that, greasing a palm with some baksheesh usually brings results.)

The first site we visited was the Luxor Temple near the River Nile. Yes, it was awesome. Yes, it was impressive and awe-inspiring if you like that sort of thing. I'm not really into old ruins, but rather locations of historical interest which hold legends and mythical stories.

So, even though in my opinion the Luxor Temple represented a lot of old crumbling pillars, to other people it could be seen as a remnant of ancient Egypt.

Next on the agenda was the Karnak Temple and this was located further out of town. The site was impressive because it wasn't in an urban setting and had a more majestic and mysterious air about it. The proportions of the place were mind-blowing and carvings were still clearly visible on some of the stone structures.

After a couple of hours our guide took us to a factory where rugs and carpets were made. Most of the workers were Egyptian children or teenagers and they gave a demonstration of how the material is woven on a very basic wooden contraption. This seemed to be a blatant use of child labour, but the boss said they were happy to be learning a trade.

Friday 20 November

Day Eleven.

7am: Waiting in the hotel foyer for our personal guide, we drank tea and watched a dubbed version of Starsky and Hutch on a battered television set. It was surreal seeing Huggy Bear protest his innocence in Arabic instead of Jive.

Our guide, Manky, arrived and showed us to our kalishe. He put the pedal to the metal and we trotted off through the streets of Luxor towards the River Nile. There were crowds of people milling around the crossing point, and as far as I could make out, only a few of them were tourists. The majority of the people were Egyptians probably heading off for a day at the office. The ferry turned out to be similar to Dr Who's Tardis; considering the number of passengers squashed aboard, it must have been bigger on the inside than the outside. As the ferry started to cross over to the other bank, it began to rock from side to side. I remembered reading horror stories of overcrowded ferries in poor parts of India that had capsized because the weight of the passengers was too great. This ferry was seriously packed – but there were two choices: suffocate or jump in the River Nile and swallow a raw sewage cocktail.

After disembarking across wobbly wooden boards we regrouped and found Manky who had hired seven donkeys. Our little beasts blindly followed one another in single file and they seemed to know where they were going. Arthur was in his element because we couldn't gallop off into the distance and leave him stranded.

11am: Food at last. An hour's break at a restaurant and a chance to blissfully rest our aching bums on some cushions. Manky cleared his throat a few times, which in English translated to: These people are staying at your relative's hotel. They are gracious, kind and humble. The donkey ride to the Valley of the Kings took about two hours. A few times my stomach lurched as the donkeys attempted to scale a steep incline but they always made it to the top safely. It made the ride exciting and we placed bets on which volunteer's donkey was most likely to contribute to its rider's premature death. But we made it unscathed and Manky tied up the donkeys in the shade created by the overhang of a rock ledge.

There was a long queue waiting to go into the Tomb of Tutankhamun, which slowly filtered through. It was cool and dank in the tomb and we filed down into the depths by way of a very long wooden staircase. It reminded me of the London Underground when the escalator breaks down.

After every flight there was a level platform to give people a rest if needed. A few older tourists couldn't cut the mustard and were panting heavily on these levels. It surprised me to see so many parents taking young tots down, as the staircase was steep and slippery.

At the bottom there was more room to move around and we explored a few of the chambers. Photographs were strictly forbidden because the flash ruined the wall paintings. Once we'd had our fill of King Tut's digs we shuffled back up the staircase to the heat and dust.

After some drinks and a pee in the Rest House, we checked out the tombs of those dudes Ramses, Seti II, Amenhotep II, and last but not least, Merneptah. All these were much the same with strange images of mythical creatures, shadowy corners and cracks in the wall. It should be said that Manky was a very cheerful and friendly guide but he must have been bored out of his head doing the same trip every day. Even so, he made us laugh with anecdotes about past tourists that had got lost, or couldn't control their donkeys and he genuinely contributed a lot of enthusiasm to our tour. We decided not to be stingy with the customary baksheesh at the end of the day.

9pm: We took dinner in the hotel and went to spend our last night in Luxor drinking beer at a cool place called El Omdah.

Saturday 21 November

Day Twelve.
Booked five second class tickets for the evening train to Cairo – Arthur would not be coming with us because he had decided to head further south to Aswan, and would not be returning to the kibbutz. We felt we needed a quick fix of cultural stimulation so we

spent a few hours in the Luxor Museum feeding our grey matter. The building was a refreshing respite from the heat of the day and so peaceful inside that it was easy to forget the hustle and bustle of daily Egyptian life outside.

1pm: We went to get some last snapshots of the Nile and then had some lunch in our favourite place, Mish Mish.

As we hadn't had a swim since the kibbutz pool had closed, we headed for the swimming pool in the Luxor Wena Hotel. Despite the cover charge it was worthwhile just to cool off. It was the only water in Egypt/Sinai not from a bottle that entered my mouth. I figured that the all the chlorine in the pool would zap any bugs and yucky diseases.

The pills that we had taken throughout the trip had certainly done their job. It was usually part of the deal, when visiting Egypt, to put up with a dodgy stomach at least once. As far as any of the volunteers were letting on we had all escaped with our personal toilet rolls intact.

6pm: We checked out of the cheap hotel and thanked the owner for his hospitality and help in setting up the excursions. He made us promise to tell everybody we knew about his: friendliest welcome in Luxor for visitors and cheap prices don't forget the clean rooms and nice food, yes, once we'd returned home.

A kalishe took us to the station. Arthur's train was already waiting and we helped him on with his luggage. Alien was very tearful about him leaving because she'd developed a crush on him. We swapped addresses with Arthur and ran along the platform waving white handkerchiefs whilst the station guards played sad violin melodies as his train departed for Aswan.

And then there were five. We walked over to the opposite platform and boarded our train for the long journey back to Cairo. We found the second class carriage and stowed our rucksacks above the seats where a beady eye could be kept on them. It was luxury not having to camp on the floor next to a hole.

9pm: There was a shudder as the train slowly pulled away from the station.

Sunday 22 November

Day Thirteen.
11.30am: Bleary-eyed and dishevelled, we pulled into Cairo. We

only had half an hour before the travel agency near the Egyptian Museum to buy coach tickets back to Tel Aviv.

We hurried out of the station into Ramses Square and astonished a taxi driver by accepting his obligatory offer of a fare. The traffic was heavy and we hinted to the driver that there might be a nice slice of baksheesh if we reached our destination before noon.

We jerked back in our seats as he shot out into the traffic flow, narrowly missing a wide-eyed man cursing us from his bicycle. Our driver was intent on accepting the challenge and weaved through the traffic with pound signs flashing in his eyes.

Memories of my taxi driving days rushed back to me: speeding to try and make time limits, nipping through one-way streets that weren't wide enough, liberal use of the horn and disbelieving waving of hands. Our driver must have been inspired by the car chase in The French Connection and was keen to live out that scene for real. It was great. The volunteers were leaning out of the windows and giving encouragement whilst keeping an eye on the watch. Time was ticking away with every near miss of other vehicles that hogged the road.

11.55am: Our taxi lurched out of an alley and there it was – the Egyptian Museum! Grabbing the socks and tubes of toothpaste that had spilled from our luggage, Frank paid the driver and we hurried to the travel agency. Trog, Alien and myself bought tickets to Tel Aviv. Frank and Satsuma planned to travel via Dahab for a few more days before returning to the kibbutz. We said goodbye, and then the two Finnish girls and myself went to find a hotel for the night. Being so weary, we didn't try too hard to find a bargain but settled on a clean double room for a reasonable price. I took one bed and the girls shared the other.

Monday 23 November

Day Fourteen.
4.30am: Awoke to the sound of the shower. Trog was drying the hair on her back and packing some clothes away in a rucksack. I just wanted to roll over and go back to sleep, but we had a coach to catch. Our days were numbered, so to speak, and the kibbutz awaited.

5.30am: The Tel Aviv coach left from outside the Cairo Sheraton Hotel, and was the quickest way back to Israel. The journey was scheduled to last six to eight hours, depending on traffic, check-points, random attacks by Muslim fundamentalist factions, and other every day Middle East diversions. I snoozed until we reached the Suez Canal. This time we crossed at Ismailiya and had a chance to get out, take some photos (now we'd left the pyramids my camera had miraculously started working again) and stretch the old legs. A few lorry drivers had a football and I joined them in a small kickabout.

Once back on the coach, Egyptian soldiers checked our pass-ports were in order. Once that little formality was over we crossed the Suez Canal and were back in the Sinai. We crossed back into Israel through the checkpoint at Rafah. Here we had to leave the coach, have our luggage checked and passports stamped, and then board a different Israeli-run vehicle.

As luck would have it our coach actually went past the kibbutz on its way to Tel Aviv. We recognised the road about twenty minutes beforehand and asked the driver to let us off right outside the gates.

It was a fitting end to the trip, and we had successfully packed in as much sightseeing as we possibly could with a whole day to spare. As we walked back into the familiar surroundings of Kibbutz Naloz it was amazing to think that earlier that morning we had been in Cairo.

The trip to Egypt and the Sinai was one of the most enjoyable and satisfying experiences of my life and I'd only spent eighty English pounds in two weeks.

Tuesday 24 November

Dan asked me to begin work even though I technically still had a day's holiday due to me. Being on a high from the Egyptian trip, I didn't really mind and went with him to the children's nurseries. Now the weather was getting chilly it was time to ensure the heaters had enough fuel for a couple of weeks supply when they would be topped up again. This would be up to me, so if the tots froze I was to blame.

7pm: Whilst I was away in Egypt a couple of new volunteers had arrived: Luke and Jez from Holland. We got chatting and Jez said that he'd spent a year living in England. He could do a passable cockney accent but would certainly never be mistaken for an Eastender. Even so, it was funny watching him try and explain to

Zero the meanings of apples and pears, dog and bone and Barney Rubble.

Wednesday 25 November

A change of volunteer leader. Rena was leaving Naloz to live on a moshav. A moshav is similar to a kibbutz, but people eat in their own houses, and normally run personal businesses to make more money. Rena was going to work in security at Ben-Gurion Airport. I was extremely sad that she was leaving but she promised to visit Naloz from time to time. Anyway, to put it bluntly, the bloke who replaced her had a hard act to follow. I won't mince words, Shimon was a bell-end with a chip on his shoulder the size of The Rock of Gibraltar. It was obvious that he didn't really want to do the job, and the volunteers picked up very bad vibes from the introductory meeting. There were some arguments and he basically implied that we had to sort our own problems out.

I had put in a request to be the volunteer leader because I was familiar with the routine and knew most of the people on the kibbutz. I was enthusiastic about the job, but was turned down on the grounds that I was not a member and couldn't speak fluent Hebrew.

9pm: I went to the Dutch blokes room to give them some aero-grammes – it was like walking into a sweet-smelling fog. They had brought half of Holland's pot supply with them and were busy puffing. They offered me a joint or two and I accepted because, well, it was the polite thing to do.

11pm: I floated back to my room like a beautiful mote of dust on the dazzling wing of an awesome cosmic butterfly...

Thursday 26 November

6am: I awoke to the sound of rain. The days of shorts and bare feet were over. I put on two shirts, long working trousers, thick socks, waterproof boots and my coat. Because of the change in weather there was some good news and bad news in being a Noy volunteer. The good news was that there was less work to do because the grass and soil became too sodden, which meant tackling easier tasks in the warm shed whilst listening to the radio and supping hot tea. The bad news was that I could now be poached to work in other, more needy places on the kibbutz such as the dining room, factory and kitchen.

Today, there was work for me in the Noy. I had to thread very narrow pipes through thicker ones. In the summer, they would be linked up in a network under the lawns enabling certain remote areas to be irrigated that previously hadn't been touched by much water. I was refreshing the parts that other weirs couldn't reach.

Frank and Satsuma arrived back from Dahab. Shimon slated the pair for coming back late and told them that the relevant amount of wages would be deducted from their cards in the kibbutz shop. That really made them quake in their boots.

Friday 27 November

4pm: Another new volunteer arrived. The rooms were filling up with people at last.

Dean came from England and was going to share with Big Jack and myself but it wasn't the best of starts for the poor newcomer.

Big Jack was in a foul mood because he'd been getting some grief at work that morning from his boss. So when Shimon arrived with the news that we had a new roommate, Big Jack flew off the handle.

Shimon: Good afternoon lads, we can welcome a new volunteer. This is Dean from England. He will be sharing your room.

Dean (polite, well-spoken, timid): How do you do? Charmed I'm sure.

Me: Alright mate.

Big Jack (throwing his book at the wall): Fucking hell – not another one! There's no room! What ya playing at, Shimon?!

It wasn't a very good impression for Dean, on his first trip overseas, and I'm sure that by the pale look on his face he wanted to go home right then. You could see that he didn't know what he'd let himself in for. Big Jack calmed down and offered Dean a beer from the fridge to try and make amends. It worked – the ice was broken and Dean lost his appearance of being banged up with two psychos in a Wandsworth Jail cell. Three people were the most that those rooms could comfortably hold but four could live in them at a push. Rotem looked a bit cheesed off at having her blanket taken away, but Dean did need some bedding. It turned out he was a party animal and fitted in with the other volunteers.

9pm: During the Shabbat meal Luke got a bit pissed on the wine and blatantly lit up a joint after he'd finished eating. Luckily most of the members had already left the dining room so he got away with it.

We told him that it wouldn't be such a good idea to smoke it in the pub. If he wasn't careful it could be a case of here today, gone tomorrow. He took our advice and got stoked in his room instead. Jez went to the pub and proved that although he sounded exactly like an Englishman, the fact that he couldn't drink ale like one gave the game away.

Saturday 28 November

1pm: It was confession time over lunch. Big Jack told me that he'd recently become friendly with one of the Russian women on the kibbutz. There were about four Russian families living at Naloz who had come to Israel to try and make a go of things. They lived in mobile caravans by the cow sheds; their new way of life must have been a breath of fresh air to them. Even though the majority of the Russians couldn't speak a word of English, they were sociable people and often invited a few of us over to their caravans.

Anyway, during the last few weeks Big Jack had been getting definite signals from the woman that she was interested in getting to know him a little better. Never one to look a gift horse in the mouth, Big Jack had planned to discreetly meet her at the pub. It didn't bother him (or her apparently) that she was married. Some Soviet sex seemed in the offing.

Big Jack wanted to strengthen international relations back at his room but she declined and took him near the caravans. He thought that she wanted to entertain him in her room while Mr Russian Hubby was still in the pub, and then nip back as though nothing had occurred. But no. All Big Jack got was a smile and a swift hand-shandy behind the cowsheds. Who said romance was dead?

11pm: Gasp – give me air! Because it was pouring down outside, the pub was absolutely jammed with people. Luckily Jez and Luke had claimed a volunteer table as soon as the place had opened, and I squeezed over to them and joined the group. Zero, Trog, Alien and Dean were seated already. Frank and Satsuma were busily engaged in a competition to see who could suck the other one's face off first.

The slurping noises were putting me off my plate of chips, so I joined an American girl that I knew for a dance. The floor was so packed that it was more a case of jumping up and down in time to the music.

I loved pubs when they were like this. The atmosphere was intense and so was the body heat. Give It Away by The Red Hot Chili Peppers came on and more people scrambled onto the dance floor for a scrum. It was a corking night and we were just wild and crazy guys.

Monday 30 November

Today's meeting reminded me that I was in the Middle East, and not the middle of Eastbourne.

6pm: Having taken a nap, Dean shook me awake and told me to get up immediately. I pushed Rotem off and asked Big Jack what was going on, but he didn't know. Outside, I could hear someone speaking in Hebrew with great authority through a loudhailer and when I looked out of the door, saw a police truck flashing its blue lights, driving slowly along one of the main kibbutz pathways. The volunteers telephone rang and Dean went to answer it. By now the other volunteers had gathered around and were wondering what the hell was happening. Was someone being arrested – what were the police doing on the kibbutz? Why the urgency?

Dean came back from the telephone and even in the darkness he looked pale. In a calm, almost nonchalant way he said: That was Shimon. He said there's a terrorist alert on the kibbutz and we have to lock ourselves in our rooms until the all-clear.

Oh, and there was I thinking it was something serious. Terrorist alert? On our kibbutz? Near Gaza? Uh oh.

Logic came into play. If we had to lock ourselves in a room then we decided to make the most of it and headed for the volunteers TV room. We all filed in, locked the door, ignored the TV and peered nervously out of the windows. We could hear the loudhailer voice periodically fading and getting louder as the police truck drove around the kibbutz grounds warning the members to stay inside. The flashing blue lights were still clearly visible.

This was mad. Was there really a terrorist skulking about outside somewhere? We were aware of how close we were to the Occupied Territories but hadn't really given it much thought. You heard about Israeli/Palestinian animosity happening all the time around the country but then forgot about it.

After forty minutes had passed we still didn't have a clue what the situation was. There had been some distant shouts and car engines, which didn't make us feel any more comfortable.

We could see the lights were on in the dining room. It was probably a stupid thing to do but some of us decided to go and find out what was happening. The girls stayed in the TV room, but Frank, Big Jack, Zero and myself were playing the heroes and set off for the dining room.

I'm sure that I wasn't the only volunteer who felt jumpy as we went out into the darkness. There were bushes and hidey-holes surrounding us and we were certain they were rustling just a bit too much. We started to run.

Zero was shitting himself and muttering in Japanese but the rest of us just concentrated on saving our breath and reaching the dining room safely. It didn't cross our minds that the haven of salads and fag soup might very well be under the control of an Arab suicide squad.

We got there and went upstairs to the eating area expecting to maybe find some police officers or kibbutz members. There was only a friend of mine, a teenage Israeli bloke (he had a really beautiful sister). He was fuming: What are you doing here? Haven't you heard that there could be terrorists on the kibbutz? This is serious – it isn't a game, you know! Don't be so stupid! You should go back to your rooms and stay inside!

I protested that we'd only come over to find out what was happening – but he was totally right. We had acted without any real thought of safety and should have taken the police advice in the first place (translated over the phone by Shimon).

Still, as we were now in the dining room it seemed a good opportunity to load up with some grub. We apologised to the young Israeli and left the dining room to carry our trays of food back to the TV room.

Some of the kibbutz dogs had joined us on our little sortie. On the way back across the grass they suddenly began barking and dived into the wooden hut that the children's climbing frame was built over. They were barking furiously inside which spurred us on to try and hurry faster without dropping any food (but we couldn't avoid leaving a trail of tomatoes and spilt coffee). There were no angry Arabic shouts, gunshots or the yelps of dogs being strangled with bare hands, but it still really shook me up.

Our volunteer raiding party got back into the TV room, locked the door and shared out the spoils. We informed the others that it was a real terrorist alert and we should stay put until told otherwise. Trog, Alien and Satsuma were stunned. Jez and Luke were stoned.

8pm: Frank answered the telephone and informed us that Shimon had said we could leave the room. We went to the dining room and the rest of the members arrived for a late dinner. There was a buzz of chattering and we learnt that a stranger had entered the kibbutz, tried to steal a car but had been scared off by all the activity.

The police and some army people were still searching but had the situation under control. Meanwhile, the kibbutz members just carried on with their usual nightly routine of gossiping and eating with their families. The incident really brought it home to me that the way of life in Israel was so very different to anything else I knew.

DECEMBER

Tuesday 1 December

Only twenty-four shopping days till Christmas. That didn't mean a thing to me because it wasn't celebrated in Israel. Still, we planned to visit the only locations to be on Christmas Day: Bethlehem and Jerusalem.

Wednesday 2 December

6.30pm: A new group of volunteers were arriving. Always eager for a free trip into Tel Aviv, Big Jack and I went with the kibbutz minibus driver to pick them up.

We were dropped off in Dizengoff Street and arranged to meet him in three hours. The weather wasn't great that day, so we walked to Dizengoff Square, by the main cinema, to the new sculpted fountain. It had quite an odd design, and it was attracting a small crowd. There were three tiers to the fountain, all brightly coloured, and each revolved in different directions at regular intervals. The fountain's dance was accompanied by music, and at intervals, a gas flame would emanate from the top, so giving the impression that the fire was coming out of the water spout. Some people thought it looked tacky and out of place, but I have to say that I found it entertainingly in keeping with the spirit of Tel Aviv.

8pm: We couldn't resist the pull of one of my favourite restaurants in Tel Aviv. The Tandoori Indian was situated on one side of Dizengoff Square and despite its popularity, there was always a table free. There was no dress code, the service was very friendly and the food was piled high on the plate, great value and absolutely bloody marvellous.

We finished our meal and waddled out clutching our stomachs. Just enough space for a quick stop at Ben & Jerry's Ice Cream Parlour where I forced down a beautiful chocolate/fudge/cookie/strawberry/vanilla/banana special. The cherry on top nearly finished me off.

After a quick browse around the Dizengoff Shopping Centre, the minibus, complete with new volunteers, arrived to pick us up. The driver introduced us: Larry, Eddie, Roger, Grant and Rosalind, who were all from the Manchester area and Beverley came from Birmingham. That brought the number of Naloz volunteers to sixteen.

11pm: I went to Shimon's house and informed him that the new volunteers had turned up and needed some rooms. The four lads piled into one room and the two girls in another. We helped to sort them out some clean sheets, pillows and blankets and told them to take the following day off.

Thursday 3 December

6am: I was awoken by a ghostly, groaning voice coming from the other side of the room. In the orange glow of the electric fire I could just make out Dean having a nightmare.

No mater, I beg of you...please...I don't want to attend Sunday School...the other children are beastly to me...please...I'll clean the Roller for a whole week...

What a deprived childhood the kid must have had. I couldn't get back to sleep and needed a piss. Tiptoeing across the cold floor (Rotem had claimed the rug as her territory) I opened the door and stepped out onto the landing. The rain was lashing against the roof and dripping over the edge of the guttering. It was freezing. There were puddles of cold water along the landing floor and I skirted around them to reach the toilet at the end. Dressed only in boxer shorts, the chilly temperature had reduced my chopper to a penknife. It was times like this when I really longed for our previous room in The Valley with its own inside toilet.

Once back in the room I dried my feet off, and put some bread on the electric fire to make toast. As it browned, I could see Rotem's little nose start to twitch before she padded over to investigate. The kibbutz vet still didn't know that we were hiding her, and although it was fun to have a dog, I realised that a proper owner should be found for her soon.

Friday 4 December

8pm: Heads turned when Rosalind breezed into the dining room for the Shabbat meal. She had dyed her short hair red Along with a black mini-skirt and Doc Marten boots Rosalind was quite an eye-catching sight. She was a very shy girl though. Only seventeen and her first time away from home.

Grant and Eddie were cousins who boxed in their spare time. There was a homemade dumbbell outside the volunteers' rooms and the two of them pumped iron after finishing work before jogging a few laps around the kibbutz ring road. They were eagerly looking forward to... a bucketload of free ale in the pub tonight, eh lads? Quite.

Larry was a nutter who relished being away from Manchester. I looked up the definition of a Larryí in Zero's dictionary and it read: Two bagels short of a Rabbi's picnic.

Compared to those three lads Roger was pretty reserved, although he had a quick wit and was the epitome of a northern student. In other words he danced funny in pubs by waving his arms around like an ape to The Stone Roses and kept saying: You wouldn't let it lie! I wouldn't let it lie? You wouldn't let it lie... etc etc.

Beverley was the mum of the group. In other words she was about twenty-eight and worried about having one sweet sherry too many.

And that was the new group. A mixed bunch, which was good because I was enjoying meeting people that I would remember until my dying days.

11pm: It was hard to tell who had downed more than their fair share of booze. The Northern Six put on a good show, but the clever money went on the Finnish girls who could put it away without breaking sweat. To shouts of encouragement I struggled to down my pint of Carlsberg, but squeezed the plastic glass too hard and it split open. Never mind – plenty more where that came from.

Saturday 5 December

The day got better as it went on. It began in the normal way with the volunteers slumped in the dining room moaning about hangovers. I was feeling fine because I had walked back home in the rain with my mouth open, and so had some water in my system before lapsing into a drunken coma.

8pm: The social outing of the week: laundry time. The laundry was the place where information changed hands and deals were made between the shelves of clean linen and odd socks. Every member paid a visit at least once on a Saturday night, and it was THE place to hang out and be seen. I was ironing creases into my handkerchiefs when Dana walked over for a chat. I still liked her a lot but those long, hazy afternoons of running slow motion through cornfields whilst laughing at soppy floppy bunny-wunnys were a thing of the past. Still, it did serve to remind me that I hadn't had a shag for quite a while.

10pm: The following four hours were spent trying to pull a girl. It was no use. I realised that it wasn't going to be my lucky night. Again.

I bought a beer and went to sulk in the corner like a wino who realises he's down to his last bottle of meths. It's funny how things can happen when you least expect it. An Israeli girl came and sat on the edge of my bench and we started to chat. She was so gorgeous (short skirt, boots, nice face, fit figure, lovely personality) that I couldn't believe there wasn't a bruiser of a boyfriend lurking around somewhere. At the clubs in nearby Stirot, I had seen girls dance all night with male volunteers – but then happily say thanks for the dance and wiggle off home with their boyfriends who had been standing at the side and watching. It was always best to check the situation first. (There's nothing worse than a violent Israeli bloke who has to get his honour back in front of his mates.)

Anyway, she was alone and the next thing I knew, our tongues were wrestling and didn't intend surrendering. Her name was Helite and I arranged to visit her kibbutz the following Wednesday.

Sunday 6 December

An American girl living on the kibbutz agreed to adopt Rotem. I had visiting rights.

Monday 7 December

Worked in the kitchen because Big Jack was ill. After a delivery of meat had safely been stored in the massive freezer, Guy asked me to grind up some chilli peppers in a mincer. He advised me to wear rubber gloves because the juice from the peppers was liable to sting.

I began to mince the peppers and paused to scratch my eye. Whoops – it might have been a good idea to take my juice-soaked glove off first. Some of the pepper juice was now in my eye and stinging like hell. It felt like acid. My eye was streaming with water. I took my glove off and wiped my eye, but that made it worse. There was only one course of action: to the nurse.

December

She washed out my eye with some drops and gradually my blurred vision got clearer. It was a welcome relief.

I went back to the kitchen, finished the job and washed the mincer because Beverley wanted to use it to make some meatballs for lunch. I noticed that she had cut her finger. Guy had given her a plaster and covered her finger with a plastic wrap similar to a condom, so the wound was kept dry. When she'd finished mincing the meat I asked her where her finger condom had disappeared to. She didn't know, but we both had a pretty good idea...

We kept quiet about the extra ingredient and avoided having meatballs for lunch.

Tuesday 8 December

Phoned home in the evening because reversing the charges cost an absolute fortune.

Wednesday 9 December

5pm: Caught a bus to Helite's kibbutz, only ten minutes from Naloz. I checked in with the guard on the gate and he phoned her room. She came to meet me and still looked good even though I was sober. (I hoped she thought the same about me.)

Helite had just returned from her army base and was still dressed in the standard issue green uniform. She took me back to her room and explained that her friend who shared with her had conveniently made herself scarce for the rest of the evening. Basically, everything was geared towards a few hours of passion.

We sat on the bed and made small talk for a while before getting into a heavy kissing session. Then she did something really sexy: she got off the bed, put on a tape and began to do a striptease in her army uniform. I had only seen that sort of thing during people's birthdays when their mates had hired a strippagram, and here I was getting a private show. Helite finished her impromptu show and got back into bed. My hands slid over her body like two hot irons across a damp sheet and then

...she got up and ate a slice of bread and jam. She explained that she was a diabetic and needed to keep a check on her blood sugar levels. Once she had satisfied herself, I took my turn.

11pm: It was a tired but happy volunteer that boarded the last bus back to Naloz.

Thursday 10 December

With lots of restless energy to get rid of, I decided to play the drums. One of the teenagers on the kibbutz was a musician and had his own drum kit in a soundproofed room. Considering it was the first time that Iíd played (apart from a couple of spoons on a biscuit tin at age four) it didn't sound too bad. Then the teenager had a turn and I was put to shame. The sticks were a blur and the beat was perfect.

Friday 11 December

It was a long but good Friday. The rain held off, so Dan and I managed to get some fresh air and potter around the kibbutz grounds doing odd jobs.

10pm: Party and punch time. We made a wicked concoction that could have stripped the enamel from an elephant's tusk. I'm glad the party was held in Beverley and Rosalind's room because afterwards it looked like a bomb had hit it – one of the drinking games had involved cakes soaked in vodka and needless to say the floor resembled an explosion in a bakery.

Midnight. The pub was rocking. Big Jack disappeared with the Russian woman; Eddie disappeared with an Israeli army girl (hang on...she looks familiar); I had nine beers too many and disappeared under the table.

Saturday 12 December

11am: Larry, what have you done? was that morning's catch-phrase. Larry walked into the dining room with his sunglasses on. Not that unusual, you might say. But Rosalind had shaved the sides of his head, given him a mohican cut and used her hair colouring to dye it bright red. Up until now Zero had held the coveted award for most radical haircut but Larry's easily surpassed it in one deft flick of the razor.

10pm: Gutted! I woke up and realised that the laundry had shut two hours ago. Big Jack and Dean had also been snoozing. When the electric fire was on it was impossible not to fall asleep because the room got so warm and comfortable. Shimon had advised us not to sleep with it on, but the volunteers rooms became very chilly at night. I woke the other two zombies up from their slumber and informed them that it was T-minus thirty minutes and counting before the pub opened. Grabbing my emergency bottle of cheap Israeli brandy from under the bed, I poured out three teacups and we drank a toast to the first thing that came to mind: Crash Test Dummies. Frank was playing their album and we could hear it through the wall.

11.30pm: I knew the bar staff quite well and sometimes they would give me an occasional free beer. It paid to be on friendly terms with the pub staff.

Sunday 13 December

10am: During tea break, Dan informed me that I had been marked down on the job sheet to work a night shift in the factory on Monday and Wednesday, followed by a day off.

1pm: Rotem saw me on the tractor and ran over with her tail wagging and little eyes bulging. It was good that she remembered her foster dad. I sat her on my lap and drove slowly along, enjoying some quality time with her.

Monday 14 December

I worked in the Noy until it was time for lunch and then finished for the day. Larry was working on the dreaded dishwasher and his mohican was like an incandescent beacon in the billowing steam.

The rain was heavy and it was cold – so I popped round to my KPs house. Mum was at home and enquired as to how things were, and if the volunteers were being treated well. She was the kind of person that would offer to help any of us if need be. I told her that our room got a bit chilly because one electric fire was deemed to be adequate for three people, but it wasn't really. (The hazy days of sleeping in just boxer shorts – and sometimes outside – were a distant memory.) She gave me a fan heater to keep for the winter months, which made the room snug in about ten minutes.

10pm: Night shift in the factory. I was working in the section that manufactured wrapping plastic and cling film for export.

Perchance you might even have wrapped your banana and peanut butter sandwiches in some. Next time, pause thoughtfully to appreciate the quality of craftsmanship – I made that. The work was boring to say the least, and I managed to pass quite a bit of time chatting to the other two members of the shift. I then listened to my walkman, and worked out how many words could be made out of monotonous. All I had to do was change the rollers on the machines at intervals, and amusing myself during the waiting periods proved difficult.

Tuesday 15 December

4am: Two hours to go until the end of the night shift. I had passed the sleepy stage by now and my body was waking up again.

6am: The boss let me go and I walked out a free man. I went to the dining room for some breakfast, then went to bed just as Dean and Big Jack were crawling out of theirs.

2pm: Checked the volunteers' mail and found a letter from my dad. They always made good reading because he included jokes and interesting press cuttings of stories I might have missed. This time there was a tape. It was a recording of him talking, playing old fogey music (we never agreed on taste) and Monty Python sketches. After listening to it I recorded my own news about what volunteer life was like and sent it off.

Thursday 17 December

1pm: Woke up and went to lunch – these recent odd working hours had been playing havoc with my beauty sleep but not with my appetite. I sat with some of the older kids who were just taking their final exams at school. It reminded me of past college tutors, and I imagined the chaos if that motley crew had gone shopping together to buy nibbles for the staff Christmas party...

Mrs Philosophy (puffing a spliff): What does it symbolise if I buy this brand of cheese – or this one instead? How do I know this cheese exists? It could be a conceptual reality of my perception. Just because Iím holding a dairy product doesn't make it appear to me as others see it...am I buying a slab of cheddar or hard milk?

Mr Politics (getting impatient): Hurry up and bloody choose one, woman! After all we do live in a democracy!

Mizz Media (warily): you're only buying that cheese because you can identify with the connotation implied by the advertising packaging. The dominant ideology of today's society targets you to purchase cheese because you think that it's healthy. Challenge it! Don't believe the hype!

Mrs English: To buy or not to buy? That is the question.

Mr Film Studies (whispering): She held up the cheese in clammy hands, but couldn't shake the feeling that she was being watched...

Ms Journalism: Quick, hot news! That same cheese is two pence cheaper in the shop down the road! Let's get an exclusive!

Mr History: Don't buy that one – it's out of date.

Mr Law: No, buy it. Then if we get food poisoning we can sue their ass!

Friday 18 December

The last Friday before Hanukka and, more relevant for us volunteers, Christmas. It was very cold but I didn't think that we'd be seeing a white festive season. Then again, I hadn't seen one in England for quite a few years.

Saturday 19 December

2pm: Dov asked Beverley and I to help prepare some of the food for the following day. I didn't realise the finger condom meatballs had gone down so well. People were putting up paintings and designs on the dining room walls and changing the flowers in the hanging baskets.

10.30pm: Donned my jacket and splashed through the rain to the pub, trying not to get mud all over my freshly-ironed jeans, white nylon socks and grey shoes. It was hard to stay fashionable on a tight budget but somehow I managed.

We went for it like maniacs in the pub. The volunteers were already in the party season spirit. I looked around for Helite but she didn't arrive. Typical. She had just wanted to have some fun, chew me up and spit out the pips.

Beer and Bagels for Breakfast

Sunday 20 December

Hanukka (Festival of Lights).

11am: I could see lights but it was a hangover fizzing away behind my eyelids. A couple of Aspro Clear soon took care of that and I went over to the dining room to have coffee with Dean and Big Jack. I resembled an unshaven tramp, Big Jack growled at dogs and made them yelp with fright and Dean looked a right state with a – gasp! – hair out of place.

After lunch I checked the mail. My mum had sent over a piece of Stilton cheese in a parcel, complete with party hats, balloons and the usual Christmas decorations. I'm not saying the Stilton smelt ripe after six days through the international postal system, but cockroaches were scuttling back into their holes and putting up Do Not Disturb signs.

8pm: A special meal to mark Hanukka. In ancient times, a pure oil lamp burning in a temple, which was only meant to last for one day, had miraculously burnt for eight. So, at the beginning of eight evening meals on the kibbutz, a member would light a candle on a specially-shaped candelabrum, until the whole set of eight was alight on the final evening.

Monday 21 December

I asked Dan for a tree that the volunteers could use for a Christmas tree. He pointed out a reasonably-sized specimen and I cut it down and hauled it to the bomb shelter that had been earmarked for our party on Wednesday. It was tricky getting it down the steps, but Jez gave me a hand. We stood it up in a pot by the wall. Jez was, after all, an expert when it came to pot plants.

6pm: A few of the volunteers went to the bomb shelter and put up balloons, decorations and makeshift streamers over the tree. Luke set up his sound system, which was pretty effective. We brought in a large trestle table and plastic chairs for everybody, and a few spare in case any of the Americans wanted to drop in.

Preparations finished, the room didn't look too bad considering it was meant for sheltering people from bombs.

Wednesday 23 December

Guy very kindly gave us some food for our Christmas party and donated a whole crate of Carlsberg. What a guy, Guy!

8pm: We skipped dinner and headed straight for the bomb shelter. The music sounded extremely loud and the confined space made it stuffy. We didn't mind. It was Christmas and the volunteers were drinking toasts and eating toast (we had loads of bread to get through).

We had prepared two vats of the infamous punch for the party, which went down a treat during the fun and games. It was murder trying to down a mug full of punch, race an opponent to the end of the room, hold onto a broom, spin around ten times and then try to run back to the start. As most of us had been supping beers throughout the day (but not while in control of dangerous machinery, kids) we were pissed as farts and could hardly stand. At one point I discovered that the floor had suddenly jumped up and attached itself to my ear. My head was thumping; the bass was thumping; it was a thumping great night.

Thursday 24 December

Christmas Eve.

8am: We sacrificed a lie-in to leave early for Jerusalem. Before leaving, I opened the last window in my advent calendar and ate the chocolate. The picture was of a golden cherub, whose birthplace we were about to visit. Catch you later JC, I said and locked the room.

10.30am: It was absolutely freezing when we arrived in Jerusalem. There were, not surprisingly, a lot of tourists swarming around the streets, savouring the festive atmosphere and buying wooden crosses and trinkets. Frank went into a barbershop and treated himself to the full works: shave with a cut-throat razor, hot towels and... something for the weekend, sir?

We caught an old bus from Jerusalem into Bethlehem, in the West Bank. Similar to Gaza, the name conjured up TV images of riots, low-flying bullets and masked youths throwing rocks at soldiers. I didn't really know what to expect but we weren't the only tourists heading in that direction. The bus was stopped once by soldiers who wanted to see our passports and know why we were going to Bethlehem. I noticed that all the time they were speaking to people their eyes were darting around out of the bus windows, not dropping their guard for a minute.

The short ride into Bethlehem took thirty minutes because the bus had trouble heaving itself up the steep roads. At one stage I thought we'd be out and pushing.

We got off at Manger Square and joined a queue of people waiting to go through a metal detector watched by soldiers. Again our passports were scrutinised. Once through, anyone with a camera had to open up the back or take a photo if it contained film. A large stage had been set up to one side of Manger Square and a banner was emblazoned with the words Christmas Choir Assembly.

We went in to look at the Basilica of the Nativity, the oldest church in the world still in use. The Grotto of the Nativity is an underground chamber beneath the church. At the bottom of some steps is the alcove in which Jesus was allegedly born.

8pm: A large crowd had filled Manger Square for the Christmas Eve singalong. There were TV cameras present and I presumed that it was being broadcast live around the world. A few other volunteers we knew were also there and they joined our group. It was amazing being in Bethlehem on Christmas Eve – the sort of experience that should be enjoyed once in a lifetime.

Friday 25 December

Christmas Day.
Midnight: This was it – many happy returns to The Son of Man. I wasn't sure whether to sing We Wish You A Merry Christmas or Happy Birthdayí.

1am: We filed out of Manger Square with the crowd and caught a special night shuttle service back into Jerusalem. We went into the New City and spent the rest of the night dancing on the bar in The Underground. It was absolutely packed with foreigners and everyone was rocking

4am: With heads buzzing we left The Underground to find a place to sleep for the night. You know the feeling: you're drunk and just want to crash out anywhere. Well we thought that we'd found the ideal place – an old abandoned bus on a rubbish tip behind a fence. It was pretty clean inside but the seats had been ripped out so we sat on the floor.

Just as we were dropping off to sleep a torch was shone in the bus and a voice spoke in Hebrew. It was a guard of some sort and he made us leave the bus. We walked to the walls of the Old City and found a row of big boulders at the bottom of a steep incline. We were hidden from any prying eyes on the pavement and road, so we crashed out behind the rocks. Apart from the summit of Mount Sinai, that stony niche was the coldest location I've ever slept in (and I didn't have the added luxury of a pair of Reeboks to use as a pillow).

7am: The volunteers stirred and blinked in the cold morning sunlight. It wasn't romantic and I wouldn't recommend sleeping in the open air in Jerusalem during the winter months. We were like icicles. Our one thought was something hot to eat.

Luckily the cafes opened early and we sat at a table in a cosy place near the Jaffa Gate. I had a mighty headache and needed a swift hair of the dog. A small can of Carlsberg did the job and was followed by steaming-hot bagels smothered in cream cheese. There I was, sitting in a Jerusalem cafe on Christmas morning, having beer and bagels for breakfast. It was one of those odd moments that will always stay in your memory.

8pm: That night we booked a dormitory room in a hostel close to the New City and splashed a large amount of shekels having a riot in the Arizona Bar.

Saturday 26 December

Boxing Day.

The first bus back to Ashkelon (our closest stop to the kibbutz) wasn't until 6pm so we lounged around in the hostel watching TV, and then went to a small Italian restaurant nearby. We lounged around watching TV in there also, but accompanied by large pizzas and pasta dishes. We ate lots of food because we would soon be back to the kibbutz menu, which didn't really tickle the palate.

10pm: Kibbutz Sweet Kibbutz. Just enough time for a quick shower before rounding our Christmas excursion off with a few glasses of pop in the pub. It had been a bloody brilliant few days.

Beer and Bagels for Breakfast

Sunday 27 December

Shimon told us to skip dinner that evening and go to the dining room at 9pm for a surprise. Wow – maybe Father Christmas had left us something in our absence? A Ferrari? Or something I craved even more: a tin of real Heinz baked beans?

9pm: A special table had been set up in the middle of the dining room with decorations and crackers, and a few bottles of wine. Guy had cooked the volunteers their own Christmas dinner, complete with turkey, roast potatoes and all the trimmings. It was a nice touch. Shimon and Guy gave each of us a box of chocolates as a present and in return we presented them with a large amount of washing up to do.

Wednesday 30 December

Some late Christmas cards arrived from friends in England. I presumed that they'd been delayed by the busy seasonal post or more realistically, my mates had only remembered at the last moment when they'd turned to inform me that it was my round at our annual Christmas Eve piss-up – only to discover I wasn't actually standing there. (Oh yeah, he's in Israel ain't he?). Nice to be missed gang!!

Thursday 31 December

New Yearís Eve.

The last day of a great year, and we were going to see it out in style. As the kibbutz members had decided to wait until Friday night before celebrating the New Year, Shimon had agreed that we could have Friday off, which enabled us to spend the real New Year's Eve in Tel Aviv.

6.30pm: Zero and the Finnish girls had decided to stay on the kibbutz but the rest of us were standing at the freezing bus stop, drinking vodka and orange out of plastic coke bottles.

The wind whistled from across the dark fields. About twenty minutes into the journey the alcohol intake had started to affect Grant in a big way.

He was dying to have a piss and adamant that he couldn't hold it for another five minutes, let alone seventy. Every bump and pothole in the road was agony for his bloated bladder. It was clear that Incontinence City was going to be the next stop.

Eventually he had no choice. Grabbing one of the empty coke bottles, Grant hurried to the rear of the bus where there were some empty seats. The next thing we saw was the look of blissful relief on his face as he filled the bottle up with recycled alcohol. That bottle must have been ninety per cent proof. After checking that the bus driver wasn't watching him in the mirror, Grant opened a window and lobbed his Port-a-Loo into the darkness.

8.30pm: Our first destination was the Tandoori Indian in Dizengoff Square. I couldn't get enough of that place and every visit was a bonus. At this stage we were quite drunk but hadn't yet reached the embarrassing shouting stage. It should be said at this point that Eddie and Rosalind hadn't really hit it off since arriving in Israel. During the meal they kept having verbal digs at each other and a tension had built up between them. It reached a climax when Rosalind criticised Eddie for being so impatient whilst waiting for the food, and Eddie threatened to...stick a fooking knife in yer throat, girl! Good job they were seated at opposite ends of the table.

10pm: The meal was scrumptious and we finished off with coffees. Grant had slumped into a drunken snooze with his head resting on the table. We put a wicker basket and lighted candle on his head and took a photo for posterity. It would be a memento for him to proudly show his grandchildren in years to come.

11pm: We walked along to Ha'arkon Street where there was a good choice of pubs. It was raining and we were cold and wet. The first dry club that we came to was Soweto, which played reggae music. I really liked it in there – but the group had its differences about where we should go. We could have split up and met up later, but we didn't think about that at the time.

Off we went, into the raging hurricane that had now blown up, and came across another bar. It was so popular, it was impossible to draw breath inside, let alone hold a glass of beer. Things weren't going to plan and the evening was turning into a disaster.

11.59pm: The volunteers welcomed in a New Year full of hope and bright expectations – as we sheltered from the icy horizontal rain outside the foyer of a major hotel. We were starting to sober up and having a go at each other. There was only one sensible choice: into the hotel that we were standing by.

Beer and Bagels for Breakfast

We squelched into the foyer and sat down in a circle of chairs well away from the main reception desk. A few elderly pensioners glared at us from their crossword puzzles – but we weren't looking for blind, ugly violence. We wanted nothing more than to curl up and go to sleep. It was one of those moments when you wished a simple click of the fingers would magically transport you back into your own, warm bed. The evening was a washout.

JANUARY

Friday 1 January

New Year's Day.

5am: We left the hotel and went into a cafe for some very strong coffee. It would have been a romantic setting at any other time: a single candle on the table, a panoramic view of the ocean, the muted sound of gulls crying on the wind. We had one communal thought in mind though: 'GO... HOME... NOW... PLEASE... ME... TIRED... HUNGRY... SKINT... BODY ODOUR... STALE BEER BREATH... CAVEMAN... UGG... UGGGGGHHHHH!'

Larry managed to hail a minibus-sized taxi and we all filed out onto the street to haggle with the driver, but in all honesty, we would have paid in solid gold just to be able to return to the kibbutz. Once in the taxi, we all fell asleep.

7am: A few brave souls went into the Naloz dining room for some boiled eggs and toast. Dan looked at my bleary eyes and dishevelled appearance and presumed: 'It was a good night, yes?'

'Happy New Year Dan...'

Midnight: After sleeping for the whole day the volunteers were fit and ready to make the most of our 'second chance' of a decent welcome for the New Year. The pub was bursting at the seams with kibbutz members, their friends, families and Americans. We laughed loudly with old mates... made fleeting new ones... popped balloons... threw olives... slurred soon-to-be-forgotten promises with arms around shoulders... Zero slipped... Frank got slapped... Beverley slurped... and everyone yelled: 'Shalom New Year!'

Saturday 2 January

We spent the afternoon cleaning the bomb shelter where the Christmas party had been held. There was still quite a bit of food to scrape off the walls and the floor had to be washed and sterilised. That cleansing act kind of symbolised the end of the festive season for us. We were content in the knowledge that even though we were in a country that didn't celebrate Christmas, we'd enjoyed the best parts of it and hadn't had to suffer the Queen's speech.

8pm: Frank, Big Jack and myself hitched to a friend's kibbutz to sample their pub. It was much smaller than ours and didn't have such a good sound system but there were two worthy consolations. It had a wood stove in the corner to warm the cockles of our heart and the beers were free: courtesy of our mate who had an extra job collecting glasses and washing them. That was the night when I met Sigal. I'll always remember the moment when I downed the last of my pint and saw her image wavering through the froth at the bottom of my glass. She had dark hair, dark eyes and dark clothes. (Come to think of it, I could only really see her every time one of the disco lights flashed in time to the music.)

My friend knew her and I asked for an introduction. She spoke extremely good English and we got on very well. Sigal and I relaxed by the stove and joked about various topics throughout the evening. There was something about her that I couldn't quite put my finger on, though I was determined to have a damned good try.

At the close of the pub I popped the question and she agreed to let me stay the night with her. I told Big Jack and Frank not to wait up and that I'd make my own way back to Naloz the following morning. They set off to hitch a lift back and I accompanied Sigal to her room. Being seventeen, she hadn't started her army service yet so there was no kinky khaki uniform to peel off. That just meant an extra ten minutes of shagging.

Sunday 3 January

6am: I was knackered, hungover and sitting at a cold, wet bus stop in my party clothes. That was the only trouble with Saturday nights – you always had to struggle to get back for work on a Sunday morning. In this case it meant leaving Sigal's warm bed to get the first bus outside her kibbutz. I tried to hitch a lift from an army jeep but they weren't allowed to stop for civilians.

7am: After a quick change into my working clothes I went to meet Dan. He told me that I was working on the dishwasher because Roger was feeling ill. That suited me really because I wasn't in the mood for any strenuous activity. It was a case of trying to concentrate on the work in hand and forget about Sigal for a few hours, but every time a couple of jugs passed by I found my thoughts being irresistibly drawn back to her. This was crazy: I'd only met the girl a few hours previously and couldn't wait to see her again. Could she be Dana: The Sequel?

Monday 4 January

Four of the kibbutz's elite volunteers left for pastures new. Yes you've guessed it: Trog, Alien and Satsuma (who was taking Frank back to Finland to be her sex slave).

It was a poignant moment for me because they were the last remaining companions from the Egyptian experience. Who else could I bore now with tales of the Nile, Dahab and long train journeys?

Wednesday 6 January

After work I gave into temptation and phoned Sigal. I thought the best tactic was to play it cool and not appear too keen straight away.

Sigal: 'Shalom?'

Me: 'Hi Sigal, it's John. Are you coming to the pub on Saturday?' (Damn!)

Sigal: 'Yeah. If I can get a lift.'

Me (desperate): 'If you can't I'll arrange for one of the army boys to pick you up.'

Sigal: 'Really?'

Me (drooling): 'No problem. I'll give 'em some petrol money.'

Sigal: 'Thanks, but I should be able to make it.'

Me: 'If not let me know okay?'

Sigal (laughing): 'Yeah okay.'

Me: 'See you!' (I hope.)

Sigal: 'Maybe.'

Friday 8 January

8am: It was atrocious weather. The rain was stronger than anything I'd ever seen in England. Suffice to say there was not a lot to do in the Noy. Dan and Galit flicked through gardening catalogues to decide what they were going to spend their annual allowance on. The Noy department didn't have that much of a budget because it was non-profit making. The factory, chicken and agriculture bosses got the most to spend because they would (hopefully) be making a profitable return on the initial expenditure. I could see the sense in that but couldn't help feeling a bit sorry for Dan and

Galit. They worked very, very hard so that the kibbutz members could live in beautiful surroundings. My KPs had told me that a lot of people enjoyed inviting friends to stay because the kibbutz grounds looked so nice in the summer months.

9pm: After dinner (I'm not saying the meat was rare but my slice was still blissfully grazing on the vegetables) the volunteers congregated in Jez and Luke's room for a party before the pub. The Dutch lads had a tape of Jungle, which I thought was absolute crap. I've danced to more melodic car alarms. Anyway, those two were in orbit around Planet Pot and didn't mind when we changed the tape.

Saturday 9 January

It was cold and wet, so we spent the afternoon playing cards in the TV room and eating chocolate cake. Zero was a very good poker player: his face didn't give anything away. Whether he was losing or taking us to the cleaners, the blank expression didn't flinch. I ended up losing twenty shekels. It doesn't sound much but that was equal to five days' wages for volunteers. I realised that I'd been on Naloz for quite a while and thought that there was nothing to lose in asking for a rise.

8pm: The laundry had lost a bag of my underwear. That meant half my supply of boxer shorts had vanished in one go. What made it worse was that unlike a shirt or pair of jeans, they weren't exactly an item of clothing that you could check to see if anyone else was wearing: 'Excuse me mate, could you drop your trousers please?'

I ordered another five pairs from the laundry shop. The woman informed me that they only had 'Extra Large Stallion Lunchbox Size' in stock. I said that I'd try my best to squeeze into them.

10.30pm: The volunteers had staked their regular table in the corner of the pub and were busy devouring plates of chips, spring rolls and toasted cheese sandwiches. It sounds sad, but that was the junk food highlight of the week.

One of the odd things I noticed on the kibbutz was that most Israelis never bought rounds of drinks.

If you wanted a drink from a mate the direct approach was the best. If you didn't say: 'Can I have a beer please?' then you would sit there with an empty whilst they happily drunk theirs and asked: 'Not thirsty?' (That's one of the characteristics I liked about the country – you always knew where you stood with people.) The pub was filling up rapidly and it was getting more difficult to keep an unobstructed view of the door. Where was she? Would she come? Why are we here? Why does toast always land butter-side down when you drop it on the floor? These questions and others filtered through my mind as I looked out for Sigal.

11.30pm: I was propping up the bar with Eddie and Grant when she arrived. I went over to her and pointed out where the volunteers were sitting before buying a few bottles of beer. Sigal told me that she hadn't been to the Naloz pub for a long time. We had a jostle on the dance floor and then went back to my room for some privacy.

Two hours later Big Jack was banging on the door and saying that he wanted to go to sleep. I walked Sigal back to join her mates in the pub and told her that I'd give her a ring in the week.

Sunday 10 January

It was Big Jack's opportunity to book into the love shack. He asked Dean and myself to make ourselves scarce during the afternoon so that he and Beverley could enjoy some horizontal dancing.

Beverley had a boyfriend back home in England and asked Big Jack not to breathe a word to anyone about what they'd done. He assured her that was the last thing he wanted to disclose.

Monday 11 January

I suffered a slight mishap at work. Dan asked me to go onto the roof at the rear of the kitchens and clear the gutter of fallen leaves. Armed with a trowel, I scaled the iron ladder onto the roof. The gutter wasn't just blocked: it was clogged solid with black rotting foliage. I plunged the trowel into the greasy mass and began to scoop large amounts over the side. It smelt bloody awful.

After about forty minutes it was done. I stood up and made a step forwards. There was a creaking noise from below my left foot. I quickly lifted it up and stepped backwards... right onto some plastic sheeting. My foot disappeared into a large crack accompanied by a snapping noise. Luckily my thigh wedged into the hole and I sat there with my left leg dangling through. I looked down and could see a couple of the kitchen girls peeling potatoes and looking up at me in surprise. I struggled to get my leg back out of the hole and saw that my knee had been cut open through my trousers. I had never been so accident-prone in my life until coming to Israel – but then again I'd driven tractors before or clambered about on rickety, slippery roofs.

The nurse put a bandage on my leg and some of that magic yellow liquid that you get at primary school. She told me to stop sucking my thumb, dried my tears and gave me a lolly. I felt comforted.

Tuesday 12 January

I got a letter from Arthur. He had travelled to Portugal and got a job working in a main branch of Pizza Hut. There were some photographs enclosed that I'd asked him to take for me in Egypt. Could that tanned, fit Adonis astride a steed really have been me? I scratched a pimple, blew my runny nose and went back out into the pouring rain.

Wednesday 13 January

I sent a message to Dan that I was ill and wouldn't be working. It was no lie. My throat felt like I'd swallowed broken glass and there was a throbbing pain in my head. It was like the morning after the night before but without the alcohol. I snuggled down into bed and listened to the dripping rain outside the window. I didn't mind having days off from work in England, but I wasn't happy to let Dan down whilst on the kibbutz because I knew that he didn't get that much help in the Noy throughout the year.

1pm: Rosalind woke me up and gave me some soup and a jug of tea that she'd carried from the dining room. She was the salt of the earth that girl.

Saturday 16 January

Missed out on a Friday night in the pub. I was beginning to feel better but still couldn't rouse myself to get up, or go to the pub. I had forgotten to phone Sigal that week so I asked Big Jack to try and get her to visit my room when she turned up at the pub. At the end of the night he told me that she hadn't arrived. I felt uneasy.

Sunday 17 January

Typical. Now the weekend was over I felt fit for work again.

5pm: On the way back from the kibbutz shop I stopped at the telephone booth to give Sigal a ring, hoping that she wasn't too pissed off that I hadn't called earlier in the week. I wasn't prepared for what I heard.

Me: 'Hello Sigal. How are you?'

Sigal: 'Fine. You?'

Me: 'Well I've been a bit ill lately. Sorry I haven't called. I was wondering if I could come and visit you sometime?'

Sigal (pausing): 'Well...'

Me: 'So, can I come?'

Sigal: 'Look, John – I think you're a really nice guy...' (here it comes)

Me: 'But?'

Sigal: 'I can't see you any more.'

Me (stunned): 'Why?'

Sigal: 'OK, I have to tell you about something. I really like you a lot but a couple of months ago I was seeing another...girl. She broke it off and left my kibbutz to travel. I haven't really got over her and don't want any kind of relationship right now. I'm sorry. Do you understand?'

Me: 'Er, yeah of course.' (not)

Sigal (consulting her book of cliches): 'I hope we can stay friends, OK?'

Me: 'Sure. See you around.'

Sigal: 'See you.'

So, that was that. I might have had a chance if she'd broken up with a boyfriend – but how could I compete with a girlfriend? It was a case of bye bye bi.

Tuesday 19 January

I was in a rare bad mood for some unknown reason that I couldn't quite fathom. Well, I had some inkling. Always the optimist I decided that now was the time to request – nay – demand a rise in wages. Nothing would stop me, and a subtle combination of steely determination and pathetic grovelling would be the key. The lady who was in charge of the kibbutz shop also handled the wages, so I stuck out my stiff upper lip and marched in.

Me: 'Top o' the morning to you.'

Lady: 'Good morning. What can I give you?'

Me: 'More shekels please.'

Lady: 'What?'

Me: 'Well, as I've been on the kibbutz a long time now and worked very hard and been a good boy I was wondering if I could have a teensy weensy, insignificant, not-very-much-at-all rise in my wages. Please. I beg you.' (I certainly took no prisoners.)

Lady: 'Alright. You can have two hundred shekels a month.'

Me: 'Done. Thank you.'

That was brilliant. It was double what I'd previously been receiving. Now the world of the kibbutz shop was my proverbial oyster. I could buy ten bars of chocolate, shampoo with (restrain yourself) added conditioner, fresh sharp razors and, oh joy, even a carton of frozen orange juice. Extravagance wasn't the word. I went wild and splashed out fifty shekels without even batting an eyelid. At last my hard effort had paid dividends. I was one of the top earners.

Wednesday 20 January

Even though I was now in a higher tax bracket there was still the menial dining room job to be done, as Dan didn't have any work for me in the Noy. Working in the dining room was actually quite a good job for the winter, as it was warm, and there were always other volunteers working there.

10.30am: Tea break. Sometimes one of the women working in the kitchen would proudly bring out some cakes they'd made.

11am: Time to lay out the food in the heated trays. Rosalind and I went on the dishwasher and took care of most of the pots and pans. There was always a constant flow of washing up to be done. It was a pizza day, which meant the trays would be hell to scrape clean. Adhesive manufacturers invest a fortune trying to invent the strongest glues they can. If they want my advice, just add kibbutz pizza pastry and corner the market.

8pm: Big Jack, Eddie, Grant, Roger and myself hitched into nearby Stirot for some welcome beers.

Thursday 21 January

I was shown some unusual holiday snaps by one of the army lads. Photographs of three dead terrorists sprawled out on a grassy hill. The Israeli said that they'd 'jumped like bunnies' when his colleague had shot them.

Friday 22 January

6am: Worked in the dining room. It was an earlier start on Fridays because the tables had to be specially laid out for Shabbat. All twelve volunteers were at the same table for a change, which meant a mad scramble for the best bits of meat and glasses of wine.

8pm: A moving, sweet, lilting song was sung by some of the kibbutz children before the Shabbat meal. It was apparently about the gift of sharing and giving to your fellow man – caring for their needs – peace and harmony. Once the song was over, the volunteers began to attack each other with their cutlery for the biggest helping of rice and gravy.

11pm: The kibbutz oldies had staged a takeover of the pub for the evening. That meant folk songs and ancient tunes. (I must admit that the twelve inch club megamix of 'Scattering The Grain, Reaping The Golden Harvest' wasn't half bad.)

Saturday 23 January

It was raining very hard again so there wasn't much we could do on our day off. We decided the best option was to stage a pool tournament between some of the volunteers and young Israelis that we knew. But the room that contained the pool table was leaking quite badly, and I was afraid to switch the light on because rainwater was dripping down from the light bulb. There was no such thing as a Health and Safety Inspector on the kibbutz. If you fried, it was just your bad luck. (Make sure your insurance policy has a clause to cover the possibility of 'death by light bulb'.)

4pm: I helped clean the pub and get it ready for the evening. That little act earned me credit for five free beers. With perks like that, and the recent rise in wages (Big Jack had also requested and received the same) my money situation was looking very healthy.

11pm: Eddie and Grant were very pissed. They left the pub, and lurched over to the empty swimming pool. Somehow they managed to drunkenly negotiate the fence and proceeded to stage an impromptu boxing match in the deep end of the pool.

Sunday 24 January

I went to the shop and got the processed photos taken over Christmas and New Year. It was expensive to get film developed through the kibbutz and took a long time because they were only sent off to the processors once a week.

Monday 25 January

It was a very, very worrying day. Let me explain...

Volunteer X confided in me that their money situation was desperate and they wanted to be able to claim something back on their holiday insurance upon returning home. The only trouble was that they didn't have anything with them of any real value. So they decided to take a day off work, go into a local town and make up a story that they'd been mugged and had non-existent valuables stolen. That would entail going to the police and obtaining an official report to substantiate their bogus claim. It made me feel a bit uneasy because I suspected that unless Volunteer X got their story watertight, the Israeli authorities would be down on them like a ton of bricks and they'd be in serious trouble.

4pm: Passing the kibbutz parking area, I saw a police van and it made my stomach turn. There were two police officers by the volunteers' rooms. Cautiously walking into my room I couldn't believe what I saw. There was a very large police officer in there looking through our belongings and kicking some clothes around on the floor. He began to search in the wardrobe and on the shelves. To say he wasn't happy would be an understatement. Tidiness was not his middle name either. It looked a very bad situation. He kept on repeating phrases such as: 'Tell me if you have drugs!' and 'Have you got any illegal substances here?'

It was extremely bad timing for Dean. He happened to be suffering from the flu at that time and was sweating profusely and shivering on the bed, wrapped in a blanket. His face was very white and it was obvious that he was totally shitting himself. I didn't blame him. He looked like the definitive 'junkie doing cold turkey'.

The police officer suspected he had taken something and kept on badgering him about drugs.

Once he'd finished in our room, the police officer went to the other volunteers' rooms and gave them the same treatment. Once he'd satisfied himself that nothing was to be found (how did Jez and Luke escape?) it was time for us all to be individually questioned. The odd thing was that Shimon, our supposed volunteer leader and the one person who should have spoken up for us, was nowhere to be seen.

There follows a list of sample questions that all the volunteers were asked:

'Your name/country/passport number?'

'How long in Israel?'

'Do you know Volunteer X?'

'Volunteer X claims to have had an expensive watch, gold chain, ring and camera stolen today by two men. Do you know about this?'

'I think that Volunteer X went into town to buy some drugs. Do you think this is true?'

'Have you seen any drugs on the kibbutz?'

And so on.

Don't get me wrong – it was not the 'bright lamp in face and beatings' routine, but the police were carrying out their duties properly and thoroughly with intense questioning. All the while this was happening, Volunteer X was being held in the police van so that no contact could be made. Eventually Shimon appeared and was informed about what was going on. He seemed (un?)surprisingly not to care that much about the situation. After all, past volunteers had been kicked off Naloz for the proven possession of drugs so Shimon had seen it all before. That didn't help us much though. (Some kibbutzim even refused to take volunteers from certain countries because of their track record regarding drink and drugs.)

In the end, the police gave Volunteer X the benefit of the doubt and didn't press charges. I'm also sure that they didn't bother themselves too hard in looking for the alleged muggers and stolen property. So Volunteer X got an official police report, Dean got scared out of his wits and the rest of us got a very severe warning and some grief from Shimon about the penalties of being found with drugs in Israel.

7.30pm: The dining room was buzzing with rumours about what had happened. We just kept our heads down and munched salad.

Beer and Bagels for Breakfast

Thursday 28 January

Time to fill up the children's nursery heaters with fuel. This task amazed the kids and they crowded around the window to watch me doing the job. It was pissing with rain, and I could just imagine the running Hebrew commentary given by the woman inside looking after the kids...

Woman (clapping hands): 'Gather round children. It's time to observe our pet volunteer clambering around on the metal frame. Who can tell me why this is funny?'

Little Boy: 'Because the wind is blowing him around like a monkey!'

Woman: 'Well done! A gold star to you. Now, do any of you know how long he can hold on like that with one hand?'

Little Girl: 'But Miss... it's only one finger.'

Woman: 'Well spotted. Go to the top of the class.'

Little Boy: 'Miss?'

Woman: 'Yes?'

Little Boy: 'What does 'ouch shit that hurt you bastard' mean?'

Woman: 'Oooh... that's a rude word that our pet volunteer uses when in extreme pain. Such as now. Can any of you tell me the meaning of the word 'pain'?'

Little Girl: 'Er – is it when you bang your head on the edge of a roof after slipping on a wet metal surface?'

Woman: 'Very good. Well done, you've learnt a lot today. Have some cakes.'

Friday 29 January

I booked the following Thursday off. It would be the third and last time that I'd have to grovel for a visa.

9pm: After dinner I went to my KPs' and watched a video with them. They owned a computer with desktop publishing software that gave me a great idea for a wind-up

11pm: I took over as the DJ for one hour while the regular guy had a break. I couldn't resume as DJ Jazzy John without the partnership of the Bad Brazilian (a legend) so had to enlist the help of Zero: the Jiving Jap. He was a technical wizard and the records and CDs were just a blur as they flashed between his hands. The only problem was that it was difficult to make out what he was talking about at the best of times, so over the loud music it was nigh on impossible. But DJ Jazzy John and the Jiving Jap just shut up and let the beat do the talking.

Saturday 30 January

Where was the time going? Every day on the kibbutz seemed to merge together.

8pm: Be afraid. Be very afraid. My missing boxer shorts had actually turned up in the laundry. I didn't want to hazard a guess at where they'd been for the last three weeks – but one glance at them told me that they certainly hadn't made it to Pants' Paradise.

10.30pm: I had an interesting conversation with an Israeli bloke at the bar. He was desperately hunting for Malcolm (remember him? – the wanker who beat my face to a pulp at the party on another kibbutz) because apparently he'd hit the Israeli bloke's girlfriend and then done a runner. He asked me if I knew where he was because there was a posse of hired killers after him to exact swift and painful revenge. I didn't have a clue but the bloke asked me to tip him off if I heard anything. That was a very remote possibility. Looking at the size of the bloke at the bar, Malcolm would have to be very brave/stupid/suicidal to show his face in them these hills again.

Sunday 31 January

Galit left Naloz. Her husband found it more profitable to set up his own business as a vet, and they'd decided to move onto a moshav. I was sorry to see her go. Now there was only Dan and myself working in the Noy which meant hard graft. It wouldn't be too long before the spring season began to poke it's head from under the covers, wipe the sleep from its eyes and mumble: 'God! – what time d'ya call this?'

Beer and Bagels for Breakfast

FEBRUARY

Monday 1 February

Pity this year isn't a leap year, because then I'd be able to stay in Israel for one extra day.

Tuesday 2 February

I saw a UFO today. Straight up – honest. Call me loony; call me hallucinatory; call me a taxi to the funny farm.

7pm: I caught the bus to see an Israeli friend who lived on a kibbutz nearby. Once there, I sat with my friend and a volunteer called Anthony on the steps by their volunteers' rooms and had a chat over a quiet beer.

The kibbutz was situated on a large hill, overlooking a valley. It was a clear night and the stars were out in force. Down in the valley there was some kind of military base but I wasn't sure what its purpose was. Those sorts of things were understandably very 'hush hush'.

8.30pm: As we sat and talked I noticed an extremely large cloud had appeared over the valley. None of us had seen where it had come from, or how long it had been there. It wasn't moving or making any noise.

You're probably thinking: 'A cloud... so what?' But there was something weird about the way it was just 'hanging' there by itself – it was unnatural – eerie even. There was no noise or movement or lightening, but the cloud just didn't look like a natural phenome-non. As we watched, a beam of very bright, white light shone out of the centre of the cloud and slowly moved around in all directions. The closest thing I can compare it to is the old, searchlights used during the Second World War to spot enemy planes in the sky. We couldn't what or where the light was coming from. It could have been a plane or helicopter. But, it would have to be a massive, silent and motionless plane/helicopter to shine a beam of light as big as we witnessed.

I wasn't scared... more uneasy that I was watching something that was unidentifiable. I'd never seen anything like it.

Yes – I've seen 'Close Encounters of the Third Kind'.

Yes – we had consumed a (minuscule) amount of alcohol.

Yes – it was dark and the cloud was some distance away.

But I still say it wasn't a helicopter or plane. That was confirmed to some extent a few moments later. Three helicopters had appeared from (presumably) the military base below. They hovered below the cloud, dwarfed by it. We were witnessing something really strange; it was the only thing in a clear sky and someone had decided to send three helicopters up to investigate. It went on for about twenty minutes and then the beam of light vanished as though a switch had been turned off. No flashes, no explosions or spectacular displays. Just gone.

The cloud began to drift apart and then vanished without a trace. The helicopters flew around for a while and then went back down into the valley. That was it. Whatever we saw was very strange. It did happen. I saw it. But I can't explain it.

Wednesday 3 February

The other volunteers didn't believe what I'd seen. (Jez and Luke asked if they could have some of the stuff I was on because it sounded like an awesome trip, man.)

Thursday 4 February

I went to the Interior Ministry in Ashkelon to try and obtain a final visa for seeing my holiday out. My 'secret weapon' letter was secreted upon my person. It was going to be a good day.

10am: Prediction only partly correct. The good news was that I got another visa. The bad news was that it only lasted for two months. No amount of pleading, reasoned argument or blatant offering of bribes persuaded the woman to give me sufficient cover until early May. That meant I'd have to see out the last month in Israel as a furtive illegal alien.

Friday 5 February

1pm: I finished work in the Noy early because Dan wanted me to give him a hand for a few hours the following day. It was going to be an important occasion in the calendar for Israeli gardeners across the length and breadth of the land.

11pm: It was a lust-filled night for some of the volunteers. Dean left the pub with his American girl. Beverley said that she didn't feel very well and went home. What a coincidence... Big Jack sneaked out two minutes later. Eddie and Grant pulled a couple of Israeli army girls. Larry disappeared to howl at the moon. The only thing I managed to pull was a calf muscle.

Saturday 6 February

Tu bi-Shevat (New Year for Trees).

A day for gardeners everywhere to let their hanging baskets down! Wave your branches in the air, and party like ya just don't care! Happy New Year to healthy trees... and a poignant time to affectionately remember those that have gone before and been made into tables, chairs and wooden legs. There was no time for wild and crazy antics though. Dan and I had work to do.

2pm: After lunch we herded a group of children around the kibbutz and planted some new trees. Then, we filled some brown paper bags with sand and put one candle in each. The children laid them at the sides of the main paths by the dining room to be lit when it got dark. Don't ask me what that symbolised, but it took a bloody long time to fill them all and lay them out.

Then we skipped around the grounds scattering leaves hither and thither and singing jolly folk songs about oaks, evergreens and all manner of conifers. (Actually I made that last bit up.)

7pm: All the candles were lit along the paths. Some of the brown paper bags caught fire and didn't last as long as we'd hoped.

I made a New Year for Trees resolution to treat them with more respect and not do silly things like carve 'JC 4 SF' with a penknife during lazy summer days in a certain apple orchard in Essex.

9pm: We had a party in the Manchester lads' room and trashed it. To be honest, it was difficult to separate the 'before and after' effect.

11pm: A few Israeli guys were getting out of order on the dance floor and barging into Eddie looking for trouble. His cousin and Big Jack were ready to back him up if it went off, but the staff behind the bar had noticed what was going on and threw the visitors out on their ear.

Sunday 7 February

Dan asked me to go and mend a puncture on the moped. Even though they had all the proper equipment in the kibbutz garage,

Beer and Bagels for Breakfast

I've always been mechanically incompetent. It took me two hours to get the rear wheel off the moped and change the tyre – a job that a performing seal could probably have done during its tea break.

Monday 8 February

I prepared the Hoax of the Century. Well, it was funny while it lasted. After work I popped along to my KPs' house and asked to have a go on their computer. They set up the desktop publishing software and left me to my own devices. I wrote out a newspaper article thus...

'BRITISH ROYAL TO VISIT ISRAEL by Avi Goldman. A senior member of the British Royal Family is to make an unprecedented visit to Israel on February 18. Prince Philip, the Duke of Edinburgh, will spend three days in the country promoting the Duke of Edinburgh Award Scheme and visit various locations of interest. For part of the tour, ten British teenagers who have won gold awards through the scheme will be accompanying him. The trip has been organised by a London-based foundation, Anglo-Jewish Overseas Opportunities (AJOO) which is primarily involved with building stronger relations between the youth of England and Israel. The Duke will take this opportunity to visit various kibbutzim in the area hoping to experience for himself the workings of the kibbutz system. The three that have been chosen are ABC, XYZ and Naloz. He will spend a few hours at each kibbutz meeting the members and discussing the work, family and social arrangements. Mr Danny Weissman, founder of AJOO, said at a recent London press conference: 'This will be an exciting and unique chance for the Duke of Edinburgh to see every aspect of kibbutz life.'

I photocopied this fake article about three times to make it look authentic, and pinned it on the notice board in the dining room with a message stating that it had originated from a recent English national newspaper. The only people who were in on the joke were my KPs and Big Jack. I sat back and waited for a reaction.

Tuesday 9 February

...and waited...

Thursday 11 February

...and (yawn) waited. Considering the fact that the Duke of Edinburgh was shortly going to visit Naloz there was a distinct lack of interest from the members. Only a couple of the volunteers were taken in by the story. OK. I admit it. The prank was about as successful as a vegetarian menu at a vampires' convention. It seemed funny at the time, or so I thought.

(But wait! There's a hilarious twist to the tale. Upon opening The Jerusalem Post a few days later, what did I see? That's right – tee hee! – a real story about a visit to Israel later in the year by Prince Philip! I know it's hard, reader, but try and stop laughing otherwise your sides might split.)

Saturday 13 February

After obtaining the key to the pub, I borrowed an armful of CDs and went to Dana's room to copy them. She had a great music system and it was really nice to spend the afternoon with her and catch up on old times.

She told me about her new Israeli boyfriend and I couldn't help feeling jealous of him for having such a great girl. It was best not to dwell on it and get bitter.

11.30pm: 'Wassat Jack? Nah...I'm alright mate...izz me own fault...burp...shoulda treated 'er better...get uzz another beer mate...hic...itzzz alright mate, I can 'old it...get off I wanna nuther beer...hic...yezzz yurrr a good mate me ol' mate...'

Sunday 14 February

It was Valentine's Day. I got a card. It wasn't signed, of course, but I soon worked out that Rotem had sent it by the tell-tale smudged paw print.

Monday 15 February

I attended my first Israeli funeral, and it was horrible.

8am: Dan and I tidied up the cemetery. It was situated on a hill out in the fields. There were lots of trees around it and it had a picturesque view. We walked around the tombstones clearing up bits of paper and rubbish. The grave had already been dug and we made sure that this area was particularly tidy.

1pm: Seven buses had been hired to transport people to the cemetery. There were lots of additional cars because friends of the deceased had come to pay their last respects. It was a very solemn atmosphere as everybody (including the children who'd left school early) stood around waiting to depart. Once the members had boarded all the buses the convoy set off along the track up towards the cemetery. Dan had arrived to unlock the gates. The crowd of mourners filled the corner of the cemetery where the open grave was, and most were openly crying. It was always a very sad occasion to lose someone who had lived and contributed to the kibbutz.

I really felt for the deceased man's children. He had left a son and two daughters, and I knew all three of them. Sadly their mum had died some years before so now they were orphaned. They were wailing and crying as the body was lowered into the grave. I had tears in my eyes for what they must have been going through. It was terrible to see friends in so much grief, but the kibbutz members would comfort and take great care of them. After the funeral a lot of people chose to walk back to the kibbutz which took about twenty minutes. I rode back on one of the buses because, for the first and only time as a volunteer on Naloz, I felt that it wasn't my place to mingle with the members.

Wednesday 17 February

Frank sent me a letter. He wrote that it was the first time in a month that he'd managed to escape from Satsuma's lusty clutches and put pen to paper. I wrote back telling him not to worry; the long, dark Finnish winter nights only lasted for another ten months or so.

Thursday 18 February

8pm: The kibbutz pub was making so much profit on a Saturday night that the staff decided to try a new venture. Every Thursday night the pub would be open to the general public, but only soft drinks would be sold.

Entertainment was to be provided by a comedian. In effect it was a good public relations exercise to keep a regular list of customers for the paying nights at the weekend and any other future activities.

Obviously the comedian told Hebrew jokes so the volunteers sat with some Israeli mates and they translated the funniest ones.

At one point the comedian noticed the translation going on and asked what was being said. Once informed about our lack of Hebrew, the comedian switched effortlessly into English for a few minutes and poked good-humoured fun at us.

Friday 19 February

Another Shabbat. Another six shekels or so in the kitty. I went to visit Rosalind who had been assigned to work in the laundry. Her red hair had faded and she said that green might be the next option.

11pm: For some reason I couldn't get into the swing of things in the pub. I only had one bottle of beer the whole night and felt guilty about it. It just wasn't the done thing old chap to waste the offer of free beer. Watching the others getting pissed made me realise how I must look after consuming vast amounts of alcohol: shouting too loudly... laughing at totally unfunny jokes... spilling drinks... slurring inane conversation... blatantly presuming that anything in a skirt can be pulled.

I went home early, painted the wall and watched it dry.

Saturday 20 February

12.30pm: Compensation. It made a refreshing change to sit at lunch without a hangover and actually manage to heartily eat a whole tray laden with food. The other volunteers sat there imitating zombies and picked at their plates like sparrows which, incidentally, still hygienically flew around the dining room and hopped onto the back of seats. I whistled a merry little tune and asked if anyone fancied coming for a brisk jog around the kibbutz. Say, twenty laps or so just to warm up and get the blood moving.

11.30pm: Back to my cheerful self again. There I was: shouting too loud... laughing at totally unfunny jokes.

Sunday 21 February

Shimon held a volunteer meeting. He asked if we had any problems, requests or anything we needed to get off our chests. There was a murmur of complaint from somebody that the wages were too small. I tried not to go a shade of red. I'm all right (Big) Jack – pull up the ladder. On a kibbutz, if you don't ask you don't get.

Tuesday 23 February

Two days off.

8am: I set out for Haifa relatively early because there were roughly one hundred and sixty miles to cover to get there.

10am: Where was I? The sign stated Tel Aviv but my bus had soared up a ramp into a very large concrete building. Apartment balconies sped by, just inches from my nose pressed against the bus window (my! – her breakfast looked tasty). Was this the New Central Bus Station that I'd heard so much about? Was I actually in its hallowed halls of shops, banks and even a McDonalds? You bet yer last shekel I was.

It contained seven storeys and the architect seemed to have gained much inspiration for its design from the shopping centre near Dizengoff Square. The new place was efficient, clean and sterile. I preferred the original bus station as it had contained much more character and life to it. But it had also contained more beggars, prostitutes and dog shit.

You couldn't always have your cake and eat it, so to speak. If my life had altered by just ten seconds that morning I could have been a national hero. Let me explain.

I was feeling hungry so decided to go into McDonalds. I bought a milkshake, fries and a McDoublecheesebeeflettucepickleburger (with extra mayo). Actually, I got two of those. Happily munching my food I wandered out of the restaurant and towards a bank. There was a guy selling some books, so I stopped for ten seconds to have a look, and then carried on. At that moment a harried-looking man ran headlong out of the bank clutching a wallet. He wasn't going to stop for anybody. Especially for the two security guards that were chasing him.

The point is, ten seconds earlier I would have been directly in the criminal's path and would have been able to throw my milkshake in his face – thus confusing him for just long enough in order to grapple him to the floor to shouts of: 'Bravo!' 'He didn't even think about his own safety!' and 'Will you father my children?'

But I was ten seconds too late and just stood there and stared with an open gob full of fries.

1pm: The bus was heading along the coast towards Haifa. Although the beach looked great, it was too wet and rainy to contemplate a dip in the surf. On the right was the city of Haifa, built up on the three levels of Mount Carmel. On the bottom was the bus station and downtown area; the middle section contained businesses, cafes and markets; the highest level known as the Carmel Centre had the hotels, posh houses, restaurants, discos and best views across the port, which was Israel's principal shipping centre.

My first stop was for lunch at the shy and unassuming Avraham, King of Falafel snack bar. (Falafel is falafel is falafel if you get my drift.) I travelled halfway up Mount Carmel to visit the Baha'i Temple, the Universal House of Justice and looked around a sculpture garden. Always tirelessly working even on my days off, I made a few mental notes for improvements to the Noy once back on Naloz.

My next destination was an attraction called Elijah's Cave, which as caves go, was quite attractive. Legend has it that the Holy Family hid there once they returned from Egypt. It must have been annoying for them to have all those people praying in there as well. You couldn't even swing a cat.

9pm: The sound of traffic outside woke me up from my nap. After an extremely brisk shower – no hot water for some reason – I made my way to the weirdly named Panas Boded Pub. The music videos were loud and attempts to strike up conversations with fellow drinkers soon gave way to friendly nods, constant outbreaks of false laughter and hand gestures.

Wednesday 24 February

I spent a few hours walking around the Mount Carmel National Park and taking photos. I decided to visit a – wait for it – museum. Ah, but this one contained art and I'd always quite enjoyed that since scrawling with a pen on my parents' wallpaper at the age of two.

It was the Mane Katz Art Museum, located in the Carmel Centre. I wandered around looking at the exhibits and pretended to observe and understand the intended concepts involved in the works. I failed, but the artist certainly knew how to splash a bit of paint around.

5pm: I had to start making my way back to Naloz. To be perfectly honest I was very disappointed with Haifa and felt that there wasn't really that much to see. It ranked way down my List of Happening Places, which was jointly headed by Tel Aviv and Eilat.

Friday 26 February

1pm: At lunch I casually dropped subtle hints to the volunteers that it was my birthday the following Tuesday. I told them notes would be most acceptable, but not coins.

9pm: The members held some Israeli folk dancing in the dining room. Beverley and Rosalind were brave enough to strut their stuff, and Larry appeared to be having a go until I realised he was swirling around and trying to chase a wasp away from nesting in his ear.

Midnight: Zero tripped into the pub accompanied by Jez and Luke. It was obvious what they'd been up to judging by the way that Zero was trying to have a conversation with himself in the large mirrors on the wall. Surely he must have realised that he was the only Japanese person on the kibbutz – so who was talking back to him?

Saturday 27 February

The worst of the winter weather seemed to be over. Even so, it was still no time for shorts and T-shirts. But it was time for a game of football! I needed to get back into shape and so did my fellow volunteers judging by the size of their beer-bellies and stubbled double chins. Enough about Rosalind and Beverley though. The blokes looked just as bad.

8pm: Big Jack, Dean and myself decided to keep the electric fire for a while longer because it made great toast in the early mornings before work.

MARCH

Monday 1 March

I received some early birthday cards from England. They were from my family, Smokey, and some people that I used to work with at a drug manufacturing company. I turned them upside down and shook them about but no money fell out.

I couldn't help but admire the immense writing capabilities of the people who designed the jokey messages on birthday cards. One of mine said – hold on, reader, while I stop laughing and compose myself – 'Have a good birthday...but don't get TOO drunk!!!' I could've made a fortune if only I'd thought of that first. The cards did cheer me up no end, because I was feeling a slight twinge of homesickness that day.

Tuesday 2 March

7am: My birthday! I was twenty-four – the age when a mature and responsible adult should really start to take stock of their lives and plan for a rewarding, sensible and fulfilling future. I got out of bed and couldn't decide whether to have eggs or semolina for breakfast.

I went to the dining room and Big Jack wished me a happy birthday, along with an assortment of assembled volunteers. It felt really strange not to be sitting there for the first time in my life eating jelly and ice cream and playing 'Pass-the-Parcel'. (On second thoughts, with the amount of suspicious-looking packages left lying around in Israel, maybe that wasn't such a good idea.)

10am: Tea break. Dan had splashed out on a packet of chocolate biccies and we talked about what I planned to do upon my return to England. I told him that the time had come in my life to return to further education and start on the road towards a new career in journalism. It would also be handy to laze around, make a tin of baked beans last a week and sponge off the State for a few years. The rest of the afternoon was pretty routine. It had been the quietest birthday I'd ever had.

8.30pm: Until now. I was sitting with Rosalind in the TV room watching a Spanish rock concert, with a band I'd never heard of. Eddie came in and asked if I could pop back to my room for a few minutes. I didn't have a clue what was going on. As I walked back I could see a group of people gathered around by the volunteers' rooms. I couldn't believe it! It was a surprise birthday party, and I had genuinely not guessed about its secret planning. (I understood then how Big Jack had been taken in so easily on his birthday.)

The volunteers were there, the Israeli gang, a few Americans and even a couple of my mates from another kibbutz had driven over. They had set out a barbecue, salad and bowl of punch, and bought me a crate of twenty-four bottles of Carlsberg. Beverley had drawn me a birthday card that showed all the volunteers in caricature form. It was really special. I hadn't expected it and was totally lost for words. Hey, thanks guys, you made a Piscean very happy!

Wednesday 3 March

I finished work and decided that it was only fair to undertake the cleaning of the party area. It felt therapeutic to put a little something back into the community instead of take, take, take.

Friday 5 March

1pm: Eddie and Rosalind had another vicious argument during lunch. It all hinged on the fact that Rosalind was a vegetarian and Eddie chose to wind her up about the way he had to eat loads of steaks back home as part of his boxing diet. He kept going on about the blood squishing out and stuff like that. Out of all the volunteers I'd seen come and go, the antagonism between Eddie and Rosalind was the greatest. She thought he was a macho, posturing berk and he thought that she was a naive little girl who thought she knew it all.

Jez intervened and tried to calm things down: 'Hey guys, resist getting heavy, Okay? We all have to live together here. Accept the other with harmony, Okay? Everyone's different. The world's a beautiful place, Okay?'

Rosalind: 'Bollocks!'

Eddie: 'Yeah – shut the fook up!'

That was the first time I'd heard those two agree on anything.

4pm: I did something that I'd never contemplated trying in England: going for a jog. It was a nice day and I had some restless energy to burn off so it seemed like a good idea at the time. I hadn't fared too badly in the cross-country races at school, but once I'd discovered the joys of sitting behind the wheel of a car, the concept of walking anywhere went out of the window. It was much easier to drive the hundred yards or so to a shop and buy your copy of 'Health & Fitness'. Or better still, have it delivered.

Anyway I went for a run through the fields and it was sunny, it was warm, it was tranquil and it was bloody knackering. Leaning against a fence and gasping for breath I remembered just how much I missed my car.

11pm: My legs ached as I wobbled about on the dance floor. Zero thought that it was yet another trendy dance craze and wobbled about next to me, grinning inanely.

Saturday 6 March

It must have been a good night because I awoke on the battered old couch in the TV room. Big Jack was stretched out on the floor snoring like a trooper. I put two and two together and guessed that Dean had probably got lucky and needed our room for the night. It turned out I was right.

11.30am: Grant and Eddie sat down with their trays of food and I noticed that they only had one pair of eyebrows between them. It transpired that Larry had been busy with the shaving foam and razor the previous night. Luckily, the boxing cousins saw the funny side and Larry was able to eat his soup without the aid of a straw.

Dean walked in with his American girlfriend and joined our table. He was grinning like a cat who'd got the cream.

Zero: 'Ahhhh – a good night, yes?'
Dean: 'Rather!'
Zero: 'Rather...what?'
Dean: 'What?'
Zero: 'Sucky sucky?'
Dean (blushing): 'I say old chap, steady on!'
Zero (winking): 'Ahhhh. You sly dog, Dean.'
Dean: 'Well – she is a spunky little thing don't you know!'
Zero: 'Know what?'
Dean: 'What?'
...and so the confused conversation continued while the rest of us creased up.

9pm: We hitched a lift into Ashkelon to watch Basic Instinct, get some pizzas and see some new faces. Watching the film, I was quite shocked by the scenes of sex, raw passion and depravity. But after complaints, the cinema usher threw the two teenagers out of the front row and we carried on watching the film.

Sunday 7 March

Purim (Feast of Lots).

This is a joyous and fun festival that celebrates the delivery of the Persian Jewish community. It's like a cross between Halloween and a very large fancy dress party.

The volunteers were eager to get into the party spirit and dressed up also. We didn't really have proper costumes so had to improvise with materials that we found around the place.

We wrapped Larry up in our month's quota of toilet paper and turned him into a (lavender blue) mummy. He said that the toilet paper was very squeezable and felt soft on his skin. I offered to swap two rolls for one of his but Larry said he was happy with his brand and wouldn't be changing.

Zero put on a bonnet, vest, large baggy shorts and a pair of sunglasses. He said he was a 'Techno Baby' – of course! (How could I not have seen that?) Rosalind, Beverley, Dean, Big Jack, the Manchester lads and myself bent the rules slightly and dressed up as 'The Snow White Twins and The Six Non-Dwarfs'.

Jez and Luke couldn't really be bothered to dress up so they just went as a couple of spaced-out, mellow hippies. The realism was amazing.

7pm: There was singing, dancing and much merriment in the dining room that night. It was funny to see some normally very reserved kibbutz members really letting their hair down and party-ing. Stayed in the pub for the rest of the night. No alcohol was on offer so that the kids could join in. It didn't matter because I was drunk on the luvvly-jubbly-cuddly-bubbly-fun-filled-atmosphere of the place. I had to agree with Dean: it was '...a frightfully good bash!'

Wednesday 10 March

Big Jack had a day off work because he was suffering from an excruciating toothache. I went to the nurse during my tea break and got some painkillers. The nurse had pills of all colours and seemed to dish out different ones every time. She gave me a packet of red and yellow ones, which I took back to Big Jack. He took one, pulled a face and mumbled: 'Mmmpphh uuurggh mmphhh yyuurgh.' One side of his face was very swollen.

Thursday 11 March

2am: Big Jack was tossing and turning in his sleep. The pain was etched onto his face and he was moaning: '...uurrrgh... give me some more of that lovely tasty cabbage... uurrrgh... I can't get enough of that quality Jungle music... uurrrgh... Arsenal for the cup...'
He just wasn't making sense.
1pm: Rosalind took him a bowl of soup and told me that he looked really terrible. I went to see him and was shocked by the swelling. The pills had not worked at all, so I went to ask Shimon to come and take a look. Shimon asked Big Jack how long he was going to be off work, as they needed him in the kitchen. His sympathy was legendary. Big Jack was feeling like shit anyway, and Shimon's attitude really put his back up. He started arguing with Shimon and generally demanding to be seen by a dentist. Shimon refused and got some more pills from the nurse (pretty blue ones this time).
I had been mates with Big Jack for quite some years and, even though he looked to be a bit of a bruiser, I knew that he had an easy-going nature. This was the first time that I'd seen him complaining strongly about something. I couldn't really blame him because it wouldn't have taken much effort on Shimon's part to give him a lift to Stirot and have his teeth checked out properly.

Friday 12 March

I was the kibbutz refuse collector for the morning. That entailed driving slowly around the grounds on the tractor and chucking bits of dead trees, cardboard boxes and other assorted goodies into the trailer. Then it was a swift burn out to the main dump in the fields and an even swifter burn back to the kibbutz. Repeat five times.
1pm: A couple of kids helped in the Noy during the afternoon to assist Dan and myself in clearing out a water channel along by the main gates. It had caved in during the winter rains. My luck was in: I turned over a rock and found a shekel! Don't ask me how it had got there, but I decided to be sensible and not spend it all at once.
7.30pm: Big Jack left the room for the first time in a few days to attend the Shabbat meal. He said his mouth felt a bit better but his

tooth was still hurting a great deal. It was obvious that he was pissed off, and took the rare step of even missing the pub. That was like the Pope not kissing the tarmac.

Saturday 13 March

It had been building up I suppose. Big Jack told me that he'd decided to return to London. He said that everything had been getting to him recently: his money was running out, he felt let down by certain people on the kibbutz, he missed his family, and so on. I told him that I didn't believe he'd stick it out on Naloz for as long as he had. He said it had been a great laugh and had given him what he needed for for a few months.

11pm: Whenever a well-known volunteer was leaving Naloz, a quiet word ensured that the bar staff shouted them drinks for the night. Big Jack got totally paralytic and eased the pain of his toothache.

Sunday 14 March

2pm: A few of the volunteers gathered by the kibbutz office to see Big Jack on his way.

It was strange to see Big Jack departing because he'd been on Naloz since July, which was a good innings.

Monday 15 March

Dan was desperate to get another helper in the Noy because there was so much to do. He asked me if any of the volunteers were interested in gardening. I told him I'd find out for him.

Tuesday 16 March

Grant joined the Noy. Well, sort of. He had his own job to do in the mornings. It was a great job actually. He started after breakfast and used his own tractor to ferry breakfast supplies and clean laundry over to the nurseries. Then he scouted around the kibbutz taking the cardboard boxes out of recycling bins. Finally he had to go back to the nurseries and collect the unused food and dirty laundry from the day before. All this took one hour at the most, but it was possible to stretch it out for the morning and then finish work for the day just before a nice, leisurely lunch.

Ha! No more! Now Grant would be helping out the hard-pressed Noy staff during the afternoons. He didn't mind and said that it would be good to catch some spring sun.

Friday 19 March

I trimmed the palm trees over by the Russians' houses and got chatting to one of the women. She invited me over for tea with her family the following day. I went to the shop and bought a sociable packet of biscuits for the occasion.

9pm: After dinner we borrowed some Shabbat wine and put it to good use making a punch. It was a lethal concoction and even the floating bits of fruit were fizzing and dissolving. The taste was out of this world... similar to a bubbling lake of sulphur on Venus. That set us up for the rest of the night and we actually skipped the pub. (I can see you shaking your head in disbelief.)

Saturday 20 March

Dean, Rosalind and Beverley accompanied me to visit my comrades for tea. The woman I'd spoken to was an English teacher for other Russian immigrants and so had an excellent grasp of the language. She acted as the translator between her family and us. Her husband was there (an electrician on the kibbutz) and two teenage daughters who went to the local school.

I have to say I felt a bit sorry for the Russians because the kibbutz members seemed very indifferent to them living there and appeared to keep their distance most of the time – I thought the Russians were polite and friendly.

The woman showed us some photos of their previous home and asked us about ours. She said that it was good to practice her English with native speakers. Considering the fact that she was conversing with a cockney, Brummie, Mancunian and an upper-crust toff, that was quite a compliment.

10.30pm: The evening was warm so the staff opened the outside doors to the pub, which effectively doubled its capacity. The only drawback was that you had to pick the struggling, intoxicated flies out of your drink and give them the kiss of life.

Beer and Bagels for Breakfast

Sunday 21 March

Dan, Grant and myself began to install the new pipes for the sprinkler system. Dan was a perfectionist and wanted to make sure that everything was done exactly right because the new system would have to last for years to come. Maybe future generations of Carsons would visit Naloz as volunteers and be able to proudly boast: 'My great-great Uncle Johnny came here and put that very pipe in that hole in the ground. What a legacy he left for us.'

Monday 22 March

I was a tad bored after work so I paid a visit to the kibbutz library. It was very small and most of the English books were ones that volunteers had left or donated whilst passing through. It wasn't necessary to check these out with the librarian – they took the attitude that we could treat that section how we saw fit.

The English section consisted mainly of detective novels and thrillers: both of those genres didn't really appeal to me. But I delved deep behind a stack of Sherlock Holmes books and managed to find a Stephen King collection of short stories.

7pm: I skipped dinner and went to my KPs' for some sandwiches and to watch the video of the evening. There were some other friends of my KPs there who I knew. They were a popular couple; visitors were always popping into that house for one reason or another.

Tuesday 23 March

1pm: Grant got a twig stuck in his eye as we were clearing some bushes away. He went home for the rest of the day to recover. Before he went I tried to cheer him up a bit: 'An afternoon lazing around in the sun doing nothing, eh? You jammy sod – that's better than a poke in the eye with a sharp stick...' Whoops.

Wednesday 24 March

A letter arrived from Big Jack. He wrote that his dentist had sorted things out and prescribed a course of antibiotics for a gum infection, which seemed to be doing the trick. He also wrote that during the trip home he'd shagged a girl on the Gatwick Express. It was good to hear that he was back to his old self again.

Friday 26 March

I went to the children's zoo to cut the grass and tidy the place up. The girl who looked after the animals, Tammy, was very attractive. I had been good friends with her for some months since she'd finished her army service. We had the same sense of humour and – yeah, OK – I fancied her. But she was happily involved with a long-term boyfriend. Fair enough. Who was I to upset the apple cart?

2pm: I stocked up on supplies in the shop. The emergency alcohol stash hidden under my bed was running low so I added a cheap bottle of brandy, which only cost eight shekels. A volunteer could easily make fifty quid spending money last for two months if they wanted to, and that definitely wouldn't entail scrimping and saving either.

Midnight: It was a foot-stomping, beer-spilling, pretzel-throwing kind of a night in the pub. The DJ was playing some excellent music with only a hint of crap now and again.

Luke had the hots for Rosalind and was trying to chat her up in a darkened corner.

Rosalind: 'You're wasting your time, Luke. You're just not my type.'

Luke: 'Maybe baby. But I can change, OK? Give me a chance?'

Rosalind: 'No.'

Luke: 'Why? You're cool; I'm cool; it's cool.'

Rosalind: 'No...you're a fool. Now give over!'

Luke: 'Whoa – settle petal. Does that mean no?'

Rosalind: 'Yes!'

Luke: 'Yes? You've changed your mind?'

Rosalind: 'No...yeah...you're confusing me. Look, Luke, you're out of luck. You're too vague and 'out there' for me. Savvy pal?'

Luke: 'Too 'out there'? I think you're mistaken, dig? So I smoke a little of this, puff a little of that. Who cares? I like you, Ros, and I know you're my destiny because my tarot cards told me at a solstice festival I...Ros? Ros? Bummer.'

Rosalind had sneaked away to get a large vodka.

Beer and Bagels for Breakfast

Saturday 27 March

A game of football: volunteers and Americans versus the Israelis. There was no referee, so most of the game was taken up with heated arguments about fouls and dodgy goals: 'You took my legs away!'... 'Did not!'...'Did too!'...'DID NOT!!'...'DID TOO!!'...

In between these little skirmishes some football was played and the score eventually stood at eleven-all with the seconds ticking away. What a finish! Eddie cracked a hopeful punt towards their goal; it bounced off Zero's head (who happened to be looking in the opposite direction) and trickled past the Israeli goalkeeper's outstretched fingers. We'd won! The Americans were punching their fists in the air and yelling: 'Whoo! Yeah! Alright!' Dean was sportingly congratulating the losers; Zero was lying dazed on his back mumbling: 'Wow...big bus! Did anyone get number?'

11pm: I was talking to a volunteer from another kibbutz who'd previously left Israel and since returned. He had a horror story to impart. Like me, his visa had lapsed by roughly a month when he'd tried to leave Ben-Gurion Airport. The security people had scrutinised his passport and asked him politely to get his baggage and accompany them to a separate room at the side of the terminal. They had spent over an hour searching through every thing in his possession. I mean everything. His radio and personal stereo had been taken to another room and dismantled for checking. They had put his radio back together incorrectly and presented him with a claims form for compensation. All his clothes and toiletries were examined. They didn't miss a trick.

Once that ordeal was over he was taken to a cubicle where a security guard was sitting behind a table. The volunteer had to strip down to his boxer shorts (which the guard peered into) and was required to present his clothes for more examination.

Once dressed, the security people were satisfied that he was 'clean'. They rushed him through passport control and escorted him to the steps of the plane (which had thus been delayed) like a criminal. He said it was a very embarrassing and uncomfortable experience.

By this stage I was sweating just listening to his account. I eased my dry throat with a swift bottle of Carlsberg.

Sunday 28 March

I phoned Rena and asked her to meet me at the airport when the time came for me to leave. I explained my visa situation and she said that it wouldn't be a problem to arrange her shift so that she could see me through without any hitches.

Monday 29 March

It was a lovely sunny day. The air was clean. My conscience was clean. My arms were absolutely caked in wet soil. Some workmen installing new lights along the kibbutz ring road had, accidentally, split a water pipe. I was giving Dan a hand to repair it with a new seal. He never complained about mishaps that occurred around the kibbutz – Dan just got on with the job of putting things right with the least amount of wasted time. He was really in his element working in the Noy and his enthusiasm for the task was infectious.

Tuesday 30 March

8pm: Tammy invited me over to watch her TV and have some coffee. It's not what you're thinking. We were just friends and got on really well. I told crap jokes and she laughed at them. Simple as that. But she was very nice, and I couldn't help but wonder.

Wednesday 31 March

I finished work at midday and hitched a lift into Tel Aviv to book my flight to Heathrow. I arranged a flight for Friday 7 May at six o'clock in the morning.

I went to Dizengoff Square and wandered around the shops for a while before watching a film at the cinema. I made the most of my time and caught the last bus back to Naloz. So I'd done it. The countdown to home-time really was tangible now. It seemed weird to think about my life back in England and how much might have changed in my absence.

Beer and Bagels for Breakfast

APRIL

Thursday 1 April

April Fool's Day. Some odd things happened.

Eddie and Rosalind decided to have a baby; Jez and Luke quit smoking; Dean said a rude word after dropping his heavy wallet onto his foot; Grant stopped boxing exercises and took up sewing; Beverley declared that seven double vodkas was most definitely her limit; Larry managed to tie his shoelaces up; Zero coherently spoke about a female he knew of called Sheila Sharples who sold sea shells on the sea shore; I embraced political-correctness.

Friday 2 April

Oh my God. Only five weekends to go.

7am: I spent the morning cutting branches off trees. I felt more confident using the chainsaw now – it was simply a matter of waving it in the general direction of the branch in question, and letting it do it's thing. Hang on a minute though – I could have sworn that bird was attached to its head a minute ago. I strolled over to the children's zoo to see if there were any trees that needed trimming, although I knew there wouldn't be. In other words, 'Oh, hi Tammy. Fancy seeing you here!'

11pm: We all got very pissed and made fools of themselves in the pub. It has to be said that I felt ashamed. Ashamed that I actually struggled near the end to finish my fifteenth bottle of Carlsberg. How could I hold my head up? It was hard, but I found support from the climbing frame during the stagger back home.

Saturday 3 April

2pm: It was a beautiful day and not to be wasted. We borrowed some bikes and went for a ride out of the kibbutz. We headed away from the Gaza checkpoint and rode in the opposite direction. It was a great opportunity to work those muscles and tighten those butts. Feel that burn. No pain, no gain.

Dean must have gained a lot of pain when he fell off his bike and messed his hair up. I was really surprised at how fit Jez and Luke appeared to be. They were sharing a spliff and went sailing off ahead blowing little puffs of smoke like a choo-choo train. We followed their trail like sniffer dogs.

Beer and Bagels for Breakfast

After about half an hour everyone was out of breath and needed a rest. We found a track leading off from the main road. It was a bumpy path, and the old bikes rattled like bones. Actually, it was my bones that were rattling. I don't suppose there's a Hebrew word for 'suspension'. We managed to find a secluded and very peaceful wood at the end of the track – the perfect spot for a picnic.

Midnight: Heartening news in the pub. The big Israeli mutant hunting for Malcolm had finally caught up with him on a kibbutz near Tel Aviv. He said that Malcolm was no longer able to pick his nose, let alone fight. I bought the guy a beer and we drunk to good health.

Sunday 4 April

The first Noy ploughing session of the year and it felt good – it felt right. I opened up the tractor and got stuck into the soil like a manic mole. Birds landed behind me looking for pickings, but I had no time to find their grubs and worms for them. I had the wind in my hair and the dust in my eyes, but – hey! – you haven't lived until you've experienced control of a throbbing piece of farm machinery. It transformed me from a meek, reserved Englishman into a brazen and confident hunk of raw charisma. I was no longer John, the mild-mannered volunteer from sleepy Hertfordshire: beware the one they call King Plough. Lock up your daughters, batten down the hatches, hide your stamp collection – King Plough was in town and rootin' fer trouble! (Just why does the male of the species change once behind the wheel of a moving vehicle?) Tammy drove by on her tractor and waved.

I impressively took both hands off the wheel and waved back coolly, nonchalantly, lazily: 'Tammy, hi. Didn't see you there. How's it hanging, sis?'

'Fine thanks. Bye.' She was the living definition of coolness. There was a month left, and I decided to go for it.

Monday 5 April

Peeping around the corner I checked the coast was clear. There was nobody acting suspiciously. I tiptoed up the stairs, keeping my back to the wall. Looking left and right, checking for trouble. I made it to the top and quickly but silently crawled on all fours to the

194

door. Opening it just a crack, I used a beady eye to risk a peep inside. Nothing. So far, it was looking good. But it was no time to drop my guard. I kicked the door open and somersaulted through before rolling SAS-style under the nearest table. In a flash I'd recovered and slid over to the opening in the wall. There was a person watching me. I tensed.

'Morning John. Do you want eggs or toast this morning?' the woman behind the serving hatch asked. It wasn't going to be easy living as an illegal immigrant in Israel.

Tuesday 6 April

Start of the seven days of Passover. This is the most significant of the commemorative holidays and remembers the flight of the Jews from Egypt. In the evening prayers were said and there was a special meal which contained a large amount of matza. That's unleavened bread consisting entirely of flour and water.

Wednesday 7 April

The volunteers had an official day off work and spent it lazing around in the sun.

Friday 9 April

No work. No pub. No problem. We had a private party in the girls' room.

Saturday 10 April

1pm: The dining room was busy because a lot of the members' relatives had come for Passover. They were munching away on their matza ten-to-the-dozen while I longed for a normal bit of soft, fluffy bread, but Zero had developed a taste for the stuff.

10.30pm: No pub for the second night. It was only a small place but I missed it.

Monday 12 April

Passover ended. Yes, I can understand that it's a special holiday and, yes, I know that it has great significance to Israelis – but I was glad it was over and things could return to normal.

Tuesday 13 April

Shimon called a volunteer meeting. (What have we done wrong now?) His news totally surprised me.

Shimon: 'The kibbutz is very pleased with your most recent attitude and behaviour. Next Monday I'll take you on a special volunteer trip. We'll be going to Jericho, Masada, the Dead Sea and Eilat. OK?'

Volunteers: 'Yeah... s'pose so. If we have to. Never a moment's peace in this place, is there?'

Wednesday 14 April

Tammy wasn't feeling very well. I put my cartooning skills to good use and made a 'Get Well Soon' card. It had little fluffy animals on the front and a cute cuddly-wuddly little – no, reader, stay with me. I kinda like flipped out into the Sick Bag Zone for a moment there. I'm fully recovered now and normal service will be resumed.

Thursday 15 April

She loved the card and put it on her fridge. So there.

Friday 16 April

'Hello old friend. I've missed you. It hasn't been the same without having you around. You're like one of the gang... no, family. You've been so – what's the word I'm looking for? – 'closed' recently. Shut away. Empty.'

Yes – the pub was open again.

Saturday 17 April

The volunteers helped Shimon to organise the equipment for the coming trip. We had so much stuff, we needed to take two minibuses. We planned to set up camp on the beach in Eilat, and one of the drivers, Ophir planned to take the opportunity to do some diving. He was a very funny guy, who taught people on the kibbutz how to dive in the swimming pool during the summers.

11pm: 'Tammy! Over here! How are you? Do you want a drink... oh, hi. How'd you do?' Tammy's boyfriend was a big geezer.

Sunday 18 April

6am-5pm: Busy Noy day. Dan knew I'd be off the next few days and made me pay with hard, honest sweat.

Monday 19 April

6am: Our two minibuses set off on the trip. Shimon was driving the volunteers and Ophir carried the equipment in his vehicle. Shimon insisted on playing his Steely Dan tape, and we allowed him that one choice. He wasn't such a bad bloke when in a good mood. We planned to visit Jericho first and our journey took us past the Dead Sea via Be'er Sheva. It's almost impossible to describe the breathtaking beauty of that region.

Pause for a geography lesson: The Dead Sea is situated at the lowest point on the surface of the planet. The water itself contains eight times more salt content than the oceans because of the dissolved minerals that have filtered down from the surrounding mountains. It is absolutely impossible to sink in the Dead Sea because of the salt. Lesson over.

We rounded a bend and saw a sign marking sea level. Our minibus was still above mountain peaks though, and the Dead Sea was another four hundred metres downwards. My ears started to pop as we made the descent along the winding road. The Dead Sea resembled a large lake and we could see the mountain ranges of Jordan on the other side. It was absolutely beautiful and became a new entry in my List of Special Places.

9am: We reached Jericho, the oldest city in the world. It is situated in the West Bank but like Bethlehem, receives quite a large number of tourists and backpackers. There wasn't much for the photographer to get excited over.

11.30am: We drove back along by the Dead Sea to a place called Masada. Now this really was impressive.

Pause for a second lesson: this time history. In ancient times Masada was the sight of a mass suicide by one thousand Jews. They decided to kill themselves rather than surrender to the Roman army and, hence, Masada has great significance for the morale and survival of Israel. Class dismissed.

There were two ways to reach the summit: a footpath or a cable car. Being masochists, we decided to walk up in the heat. It was harder than we'd first envisaged, but Israeli soldiers march up Masada in full kit as part of their training. How they do it, I'll never know.

We reached the summit in under an hour. We could just make out the outline of old Roman camps at the base. The fortress itself was pretty much intact, and we took photos of the chambers and mosaics.

After having our fill of Masada, we took the easy option and caught the cable car down. We met up with Ophir and drove to the Ein Gedi camping site just down the road to stay overnight.

Tuesday 20 April

After a very muggy night's sleep we were just about ready to tackle the Ein Gedi Nature Reserve. It was a literal oasis in the desert and we swam under the waterfalls. The water was clean, cool and refreshing.

1pm: A float in the Dead Sea. Some of the nicer beaches had to be paid for but we went to a free one and stripped down to the bare essentials. The sun was dazzling on the columns of hardened white salt and if it hadn't been so hot it could have been a scene straight from the Arctic.

I gingerly picked my way over the stones and slid into the Dead Sea. The water was very warm and supported my body with no trouble at all. It was the weirdest feeling not to sink. You could even float in an upright position and hold your hands above your head. I copied the swarms of tourists and had a photo taken, lying back and reading a newspaper. (Well, it had to be done.)

I had cut my leg climbing up Masada and the water made it sting like hell. My bell-end was sore too from the salt.

At one point a drop of water splashed into my eye. It was searing. I got out and rinsed my eye under one of the showers. It must be agony to have your whole head shoved under the surface and swallow a mouthful. There was a large container on the beach full of Dead Sea mud. The volunteers smothered each other in it and let it dry hard under the sun. Apparently the foul-smelling mud was good for the skin, ducky. I rinsed it off under a shower and – yes – my skin did have a pleasing, tingling glow to it. We floated around some more and then thoroughly washed the greasy, oily water off our bodies. I didn't want a layer of itchy salt underneath my clothes during the long drive to Eilat.

4pm: I experienced one of my lasting memories of the holiday. It may not sound very special but it was for me. We drove along through the desert towards Eilat. The heat was shimmering outside on the flat expanse. 'Riders On The Storm' by The Doors trickled out of the speakers. It was captivating.

8pm: Hello Eilat. We picked a spot on the beach near Taba for the volunteers' base camp. We spent the evening erecting the large tent and setting up the stove, fridge (yes – we had all the luxuries), tables, chairs and larder. Then we cooked dinner and had some beers. The sea lapped lazily at the shore a few metres from our sleeping bags. It was heaven.

Wednesday 21 April

8am: I awoke to the sound of the sea and the radio. Shimon was preparing breakfast and the smell of scrambled eggs wafted up my nostrils. The volunteers were beginning to stir and rubbing their bleary eyes. Zero had been up for ages and was practising his T'ai Chi exercises on the sand.

After breakfast we did some diving. Ophir gave out masks and snorkels and told us to wear sandals in the water because there could be nasty spiky animals that hid in the coral.

The water of the Red Sea was crystal-clear and teeming with fish. I floated out over one large mass of coral and suddenly the sea floor dropped away and I was staring down into an abyss. It was awesome but I didn't want to dive down and see what might be lurking in its depths. I could only plunge to a certain depth before my ears began to squeal and my eyes pop. It was like another world under there. Ophir had the full diving kit on and was happily gliding around at a much greater depth.

2pm: We drove along the coast to the Coral World Underwater Observatory and Aquarium. It was very interesting but, in all honesty, I've never really enjoyed seeing animals in captivity. Rosalind felt the same way and didn't even want to go in.

Beer and Bagels for Breakfast

10pm: Larry and I went to Sheba's, my favourite club in Eilat. The other volunteers had decided to stay at the bar that was right next to our camp on the beach. By the time we caught a taxi back to the camp most of the volunteers had crashed out for the night.

Thursday 22 April

We spent the day on the main beach in Eilat. A woman offered me a job serving in a bar but I had to decline. I got the distinct impression that work was easy to find in Eilat if you looked hard enough and were prepared to be flexible. Eddie, Grant, Larry and myself decided to have a go at parasailing. It was to be one of the most painful things I've ever attempted. We headed out into the bay on the boat that would tow us, and Grant went first, followed by Eddie, who both did very well and enjoyed it enormously.

Next, it was my turn. Paragliding essentially involves being towed behind a boat, with a parachute on your back, whilst the line connecting you is winched out so that you float high above the water. Straps are fastened across your chest and through your legs forming a kind of 'seat' that is meant to support your backside. Things started well and I got up to a good height. The view was spectacular, stretching out to the beach and beyond. But the wind picked up, and I began to get blown from side to side. One of the straps started to slip, and it trapped one of my bollocks. It tightened and cut off the blood supply to my testicles. It goes without saying that it hurt, and as I had always planned to be a father at some stage, I decided to cut my ride short, which was easier said than done.

I was pretty high up, and the wind was carrying the words out of my mouth and off to sea. I tried to signal to the captain, but he misinterpreted my frantic waving and cheerfully returned a wave. He couldn't see how much my eyes were watering. So I tried making cutting gestures across my throat: GET ME DOWN!! Eddie must have realised that I wasn't too happy and I saw him speak to the captain.

Then slowly... slowly... slowly I was winched back into the boat. The harness was unfastened and I lay on my back taking deep breaths. The pain in my groin was excruciating and I seriously thought that I'd been permanently damaged in some way, but a few minutes later the blood rushed back in and it wasn't so bad. I would never try parasailing again.

Larry had a hideous calamity. He was being winched up when a gust of wind blew him back down into the sea. The only way to get him out was for the captain to increase the speed of the boat and create a lift to raise his parachute up again. Unfortunately, Larry was being dragged through the sea and it must have appeared from the shore that we were engaged in a spot of shark fishing using human bait.

10pm: Larry and I persuaded the other volunteers to try an evening at Sheba's. It didn't work out quite as planned. Only half of the group was let in by the bouncers. That wasn't on, so we got our entrance fee back and returned to the camp, which turned out to be a stroke of luck. Unbeknown to us, the bar held a huge beach rave every Thursday night. We grabbed a beer and joined them. Jez and Luke both dropped some acid they'd been sent by a mate in Holland, and spent most of the night playing a game of 'Cowboys and Indians' in and around the boulders on the beach.

Friday 23 April

6am: The rave was just coming to a close and only Larry, Rosalind and myself had gone the distance. The others were huddled in their sleeping bags further down the beach at the camp. Raving on a beach while watching the sunrise catch the mountains of Jordan across the Red Sea would be a lasting memory of this holiday. I had no desire to sleep – I was on a high, and without beer – it was the first time I'd ever partied so long without alcohol. Rosalind and Larry were also still going strong and prepared to dance on, but the bar had shut and the rave was over.

We walked back to the camp and made some strong coffee and got breakfast ready. They didn't realise that we hadn't been asleep. Dean said that the thumping music had kept him awake all night but he'd been too tired to join the rave. I was just glad that I had seen it through to the end.

11am: We packed the equipment and enjoyed a last swim. Then we boarded the minibuses and set off for the long drive back to Naloz. This last volunteer trip had definitely been the best.

Saturday 24 April

During lunch the volunteers reminisced about the trip. I realised that there were only two places in Israel that I'd wanted to visit but hadn't had the time or opportunity. They were Nazareth and Megiddo, the latter being the alleged location for the end of the world. Whoooo!

I was happy with the places I'd visited; Tel Aviv, Eilat and the Dead Sea were the best. I'm sorry citizens of Haifa – but your city got the wooden spoon.

10.30pm: I was well aware that every time I did something now on the kibbutz it could be for the last time. There were still four pub nights left and I made sure that I savoured every one.

Sunday 25 April

Memorial Day in Israel. The country remembered people who had given their lives in Israel's many wars. The sirens sounded on the kibbutz for two minutes whilst everyone stood in silence.

Monday 26 April

In contrast, Independence Day was a celebration. No work and the pub was open.

Tuesday 27 April

Dan asked me to shape the large bushes that were planted around the main office. I made sure that there wasn't a leaf out of place. Birds took one look at my glare of warning and were afraid to land on them.

10pm: I went to see Tammy. Whilst in Eilat I'd bought a picture for her to put on the wall. Israelis went totally over the top when you gave them presents and Tammy was no exception. I mean, it was only a picture, but I was glad that she liked it. For some reason I felt really shy to be with her, which was unusual as we normally got on great. There was a tense, expectant atmosphere as she made some coffee. I watched her television but my concentration was all over the place.

She walked back over, said thanks again for the picture and gave me an appreciative kiss. To my genuine surprise it wasn't just a peck on the cheek. It was a red-blooded snog! I was really stunned and could only bluster about like a moron. Deep and meaningful words failed me: 'Er, thanks. So you liked it then?' (What a prat.) Tammy: 'Of course.'

She was playing it very cool and I was wasting time. I just couldn't push it any further and have always regretted letting that moment slip by. Anyway, we chatted for a while until it was time for me to go. With one last look at her big, empty bed I left the room...

...and she followed. Tammy said that she'd like to walk back with me. It's easy to write about it now but something was holding me back that night. I've never been able to work out exactly what it was. Maybe my subconscious was letting me know that in a week or so I'd be leaving the kibbutz and didn't want to make it any harder than it was already going to be.

Tammy and I walked back to the volunteers' rooms and sat on the climbing frame. It was a warm and silent night. There was nobody else around. We talked, had a very hot kissing and cuddling session, she told me that she liked me... I asked her to give her boyfriend up, she said that only long-term relationships appealed to her... she meant a lot to me but I had to catch that flight home.

So that was that. We enjoyed some time together but it never went any further. Maybe if I'd met her at the start of my kibbutz year things might have turned out differently.

Wednesday 28 April

It was time to strap on the strimmer and strive to strip the shrubs and... strewth! Those weren't weeds – they were Triffids.

The blade didn't have a guard on it and all the bits of leaf and stalk were sprayed back at me. I sprouted a green beard and was soon covered in grass. It was useful though because kids were unable to spot me camouflaged in front of the bushes and I could jump out on them and shout: 'BOO! THE BUSH MONSTER'S GOING TO GET YOOOO!!' They just laughed at my pathetic attempts to scare them. Then beat me up for something to do.

Thursday 29 April

Zero's birthday. He felt very homesick so we arranged a party and barbecue. Guy donated some meat and we bought the rest of the supplies from the shop. A few of the Americans turned up with vodka. Even Montgomery Jnr showed his face. Since Big Jack had left the kibbutz he'd resorted back to his old ways and acted like he owned the place. Eddie and Grant had heard all about Montgomery Jnr and warned him: 'You fookin' mess with us pal and see what you fookin' get. Alright?'

Montgomery Jnr suddenly remembered that he had a prior engagement and scurried off. That was one arsehole who really put my back up. He treated the volunteers like shit and we weren't going to stand for it. Zero was in his element. The vodka had reached his brain and was affecting his mouth.

Zero: 'Great party! Nice food! Get down on it!'

Dean: 'I say, Zero. Save me some of the old Soviet juice.'

Jez: 'Yeah steady on, Z. The beer collection's getting a bit low. Hey John – haven't you got some brandy, man?'

Me: 'Oh yeah.' (Damn.)

Larry: 'Jesus, that sausage was hot. Hey look at Rotem dancing about! She's got it stuck in her mouth!'

Rosalind: 'Quick Larry – get it out!'

Larry: 'Beg your pardon?'

Rosalind: 'Get your sausage out NOW!'

Luke: 'Hey Ros... Can I get mine out?'

Rosalind: 'Sorry mate. I'm a vegetarian.'

Zero: 'Jingle balls, jingle balls...'

Friday 30 April

I helped Dan make repairs to the Noy greenhouse. It wasn't a proper greenhouse but the plastic that covered the walls and roof had tears in them since the last inspection. It was simply a matter of getting a hammer and tacks and securing the plastic sheeting back into place. After tea break, I went to an old lady's house to cut down a small tree that was blocking the light from her window. She couldn't speak a word of English but supplied me with tea and cakes. I know it was an easy life for old people on the kibbutz but they must have been very bored. All they seemed to do was sit outside their houses or plan a timetable for setting off for the dining room when it was nearly time to eat. 'Nearly' in their case meant three hours.

8pm: I looked across the table at my KPs. It was my last Shabbat meal and I felt it only right to sit with the people who had helped me the most throughout my stay. In the absence of a Carlsberg brewer that meant Assaf and Anat. My little kibbutz brother looked up at me with sad eyes and I playfully ruffled his hair, dislodging the spaghetti that he'd stuck there earlier. It seemed inappropriate to nick any bottles of wine from my last Shabbat meal so I downed a couple at the table instead. My kibbutz mum couldn't conceal her astonishment at the amount I'd drunk.

'I'm sorry,' I explained. 'The bread filled me up.'

11pm: It was overwhelming. The volunteers generously bought me free beers all night. (Hang on? Isn't it Friday night? Crafty little whippersnappers.)

Beer and Bagels for Breakfast

MAY

Saturday 1 May

A new month. A new beginning. The healthy kibbutz life had got
to me and I relished munching away at my food after a good night
in the pub. Mmmmm... get a load of that green bean salad. Pass the
mineral water will you? Be careful, your elbow nearly contaminated
my nut cutlet. I was a new person. Fit and healthy. Ready for
anything. Junk food? Fattening sweets? Lard? Don't make me laugh,
pal.

2pm: It was time to play football and show those Israelis who's
boss. I limbered up and ran a few laps before the game. It felt natural. My body had developed into a lean and powerful vision of
muscle, sinew and gristle.

My hands were lethal weapons of death... my eyes scouted for
trouble... my reflexes faster than a fiddler's elbow. The volunteers
won the game easily. I cheered from the sidelines because I'd
stubbed my toe and had to call it a day.

8pm: I walked slowly around the laundry collecting the last of
my clean washing. It brought back fond memories... I smiled as I
noticed my old boots I'd worn whilst working in the cow sheds.
Huh...we've certainly been through some shit together you and I,
eh?

10.30pm: This was it. My final evening in the Naloz pub.

Stringfellows...Vegas...The Grimsby Social Club – I'd been to
some wild and crazy places in my time but the Naloz pub would
always hold a special place in my heart. I relished my last plate of
chips and chewed each one twice to make the pleasure last longer.
I went to the bar: 'What's that? Free beers all night? You shouldn't
have...no, really, it's too much...how could I? Pardon? No it's alright.
I was only joking. Alright then, if you insist. Carlsberg please.'
(Nearly overplayed my hand there.)

I said goodbye! ciao! au revoir! to volunteer friends of all nation-
alities from other kibbutzim that I spotted during the evening.
Bonds had been formed; friendships sealed; embarrassing records
danced to. Who cared? Did it matter? Was it that sad? (Yes, the
photographic evidence was actually.)

The memories flooded back. There was the bar stool that Ben
had hit his head on after drunkenly falling over... the table where
Trog had downed that pint in one and then sprayed it from her
nose... the dance floor where we'd premiered the Ace of Base

Beer and Bagels for Breakfast

(currently at all good clubs near you). Happy times.

I got drunk, waved my arms in the air and partied like I just didn't care. But this time I did. I'd really miss the place.

Sunday 2 May

After work I went to the kibbutz shop and closed my account. Being thirty shekels in the red I settled with the woman and signed my card over. I no longer officially existed on the kibbutz.

Monday 3 May

Grant worked with me in the Noy for the whole day. He was going to be taking over my job as sole gardening volunteer. I showed him the basics of where things were kept, how to service the cutting machines and – most importantly – how to make mud coffee the way that Dan liked it. It paid to keep the boss happy.

Tuesday 4 May

Dean took a last photo of me in the room before I packed my luggage. Larry was going to move in once I'd gone.

Wednesday 5 May

I commandeered the tractor for the whole day and made the most of riding around. The following day it was going to the garage for a complete overhaul. Grant would be inheriting a pretty nifty set of (ribbed) wheels.

4pm: 'Goodbye old son. You haven't let me down. Reliable and not afraid of a bit of hard work. Not like those fancy Italian jobs with their air-conditioned cabs and padded seats. No – you can't beat having no roof... or windscreen... or doors. Try not to strain your old engine or hit a ditch. You're one of the best. Gawd bless yer!' I patted the tractor and walked away into the distance.

7pm: I skipped dinner and went to my KPs' house. Anat was overjoyed with the framed picture that I'd bought for her son as a 'thank you'. You definitely couldn't go wrong with a bit of artwork. She wiped away her tears, and finished chopping the onions for dinner.

May

Thursday 6 May

Dan said I could have the day off but I wanted to work. During the tea break he thanked me for all I'd done in the Noy and gave me a t-shirt, baseball cap and a box of chocolates. I thanked him and said that now I was able to impress the folks back home with my botanical knowledge.

Then we laughed about the good times (burning old trees whilst watching the animals run for cover) and scowled at the bad times (the pipe I'd broken that had turned the Noy yard into a river of mud). We laughed and scowled until it was time to resume work.

4pm: I phoned Rena to confirm that she would be at the airport to save my skin. Her mum answered and I asked her to pass on the message. Please. Don't forget now. Okay?

7pm: I went around the dining room saying goodbye to the people I knew and the friends I'd made.

'Bye Beatrice. I'm glad we became mates. A volunteer should never forget their first leader.'

'Bye Guy. Yeah, let's shake to the future... Ow! You're crushing my hand! Let go!'

'Bye Uncle Dov. I was only joking about the goat with no name and women's clothing. I'm glad you can laugh about it. No, of course I won't... your other secret's safe with me, mate.'

'See you later Shimon. OK I have to agree with you, we didn't hit it off at first. Let's part friends. Do me a favour though: shave off that crap beard. It looks like a ferret that an elephant's farted out. Pardon? Oh, a furry little creature. Yeah. Ha ha. Good one.'

'Goodbye Dan. Thanks for everything. It's been great. You've been like a boss to me.'

'Dana. Come here and give me a hug. Yeah so will I. Don't worry of course I will. Here's my address too. Married? When? Oh well, all the best then. Try not to compare him to me on your wedding night.'

'Take care Tammy. What? People are watching? So what – friends can hug can't they? No... it's a bun in my pocket. For the journey. I might get hungry.' (Only for you.)

11pm: I walked out of the volunteers' accommodation blocks for the last time. The others had made a little arch and were waving their lighters around in a mock ceremony. I said goodbye to them and anxiously looked around. Where was she? Had she forgotten I was leaving? No! She came running over. Her brown eyes were watering and she was out of breath. I dropped my luggage and hugged her: 'Goodbye Rotem. Don't chase too many parked tractors.'

My Israeli mate from Kibbutz Gerim had arrived in a car. He'd generously agreed to give me a lift to Ben-Gurion Airport. I loaded my luggage, waved one last time to the gathered volunteers and we drove out of the place that had been my home for the last year. I absently noticed that one of the young trees by the gate needed trimming back a touch.

Friday 7 May

3am: My friend had left, and I was waiting to check in at the airport. I frantically looked around for Rena. Had she got the message? What if she didn't turn up? I needn't have worried. She spotted me and came over. She looked pretty sexy in her official security outfit.

By whisking me through the security checks, Rena was placing a lot of trust in me. Her job could have been on the line if I'd abused it. She took me to one side and asked if there was anything in my luggage that might cause a surprise.

'Only this!' I said, giving her a necklace. She loved it.

Then she slapped a red sticker on my luggage and the security guards waved me through without so much as a question. We went to have a last chat over some coffee. Rena was really a very special person and a good friend.

7am: And here I am. Sitting in my seat, having my back kicked by the kids behind me as my plane climbs up over the clouds into the sun. England awaits. I think of the excellent memories I have to take back with me: Einar killing and eating a chicken... chasing cows... terrorist alerts... Jerusalem... Egypt... great parties... belly dancers... good laughs.

Whilst I imagined it would be a challenge to recount them for whoever is interested, after all one person's ideal could be another's ordeal, three things are certain.

1) If you decide to spend any time as a volunteer you will not regret it and will meet some fantastic people.

2) Keep an open mind and do not be afraid to try any challenge, job or alcoholic drink that comes your way.

3) Everything you have read really happened. Your holiday might be better or worse.

And there is one other important piece of advice, which might make all the difference...

But on second thoughts, I think you should find out for yourself.

Beer and Bagels for Breakfast